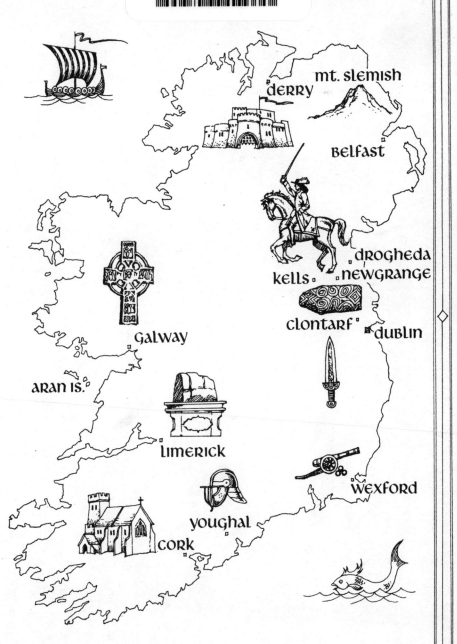

mt. slemish

derry

belfast

dRogheda

kells · · newgrange

clontarf · dublin

Galway

aran is.

limerick

youghal

cork

wexford

the story of ireland

the story of IReLand

episodes from Irish history

Michael Scott

*Illustrated by
Hemesh Alles*

DENT CHILDREN'S BOOKS
London

For Max Morgan Walsh – a little piece of history

First published in 1990
Text copyright © Michael Scott, 1990
Illustrations copyright © Hemesh Alles, 1990

Printed in Great Britain by The Bath Press Ltd, Avon,
for J.M.Dent & Sons Ltd
91 Clapham High Street
London SW4 7TA

British Library Cataloguing in Publication Data
Scott, Michael
The story of Ireland.
I. Title
823'.914 [J]

ISBN 0-460-88046-2

contents

preface

People make history.

Sometimes, with all the dates and facts and figures, it is easy to forget that ordinary – and not-so ordinary – people took part in those events in the past which shape the present. Some fought and died, others merely looked on. Yet whatever they did, each person became part of history, with his or her personal memories of what had taken place.

The following collection of stories is nothing more than the memories of people looking back on or living through what we call history. Their tales make up part of the Story of Ireland . . .

NEWGRANGE

Newgrange is Ireland's finest ancient monument and one of the most famous burial sites in Europe. It was built more than three thousand years before the birth of Christ by farmers, using simple tools, and yet it is a hugely complex structure, made from over 180,000 tons of stone.

No one knows exactly why it was built. Certainly, the Druid priesthood used Newgrange as a place of worship for centuries, and there is evidence that it had been a burial site before that. Was some great king buried there and the huge mount raised over his grave as a memorial? And did this king in time become a god? In ancient times the monument was called Bru na Boinne, the House of the Boyne, and was believed to be the home of the gods.

Newgrange is a strange and wild place. It is older than Stonehenge, older than the pyramids of Egypt ... and just as mysterious.

The rain had ceased and the clouds rolled away, leaving the sky clear, with the stars sparkling bright and sharp. There were people moving about, vague shapes and muffled noises in the darkness, but, although it was cold and there was a chill wind whistling in from the north, there were no fires or lights burning. It was Midwinter's Eve, a special time in the ancient forested land that would one day be called Ireland.

9

Sitting in the shelter of one of the tall standing stones that dotted the field, Mura moved closer to his father, both for warmth and comfort. This was the first time he had come to the House of the Dead and he was frightened.

Conn, his father, put an arm around his son's shoulders and hugged him close. 'There's nothing to fear,' he said softly, his voice not rising above a whisper.

'Will the dead walk?' the boy asked, looking across towards the high white-walled mound on the far side of the field. Even though it was after midnight, the hillock still seemed bright, far too bright.

'I've never seen them,' his father replied quietly. Although he was not an old man, Conn was an elder of the tribe, one of those whose task it was to keep the ancient traditions alive and pass on their knowledge to the young. One of his duties was to attend to the great burial site, keeping it free from weeds and the tough, sharp-edged grass. And every year for the past fifteen years, he had led his people to the mount on the eve of Midwinter, so that they could see for themselves the great mystery of the place. This year his son was in his thirteenth year, on the verge of manhood; eventually he, too, would become an elder of the tribe, and it would be his turn to safeguard the legends of their people. Tonight, he would learn the secret of the Bru na Boinne.

'But that doesn't mean the dead *won't* ride out,' Mura persisted.

Conn nodded, unable to argue with his son; just because something had not happened in his lifetime didn't mean that it never would. He glanced up into the heavens, judging the time by the position of the stars. Morning – and more importantly, sunrise – was still a little way off. He looked across the field towards the mound, feeling once again the strange eerie chill he always experienced when he came to this sacred place. This was Bru na Boinne, the House of the Boyne. If he listened carefully, he could hear the river Boyne singing softly to itself a little to the south, the sound carried clearly on the still night air. Conn smiled, remembering the time *his* father had first brought him to this place, many years ago. Then he had thought the sound of the not-so distant river to be people – spirits, gods, the dead – whispering together inside the man-made hill.

'Father,' Mura asked, his voice soft and frightened, 'who built this place?'

'I can tell you the tales or the truth,' Conn said, bending down his head so that no one else could hear. 'But I should warn you that it's sometimes difficult to tell one from the other. Now, which do you wish to hear?'

'Tell me the tales,' the boy said without hesitation. Mura love the ancient tales and legends, and Conn knew that his son had the makings of a bard, or story-teller. Yet even now, although he was only twelve, Mura was already too old to be apprenticed to a bard.

Looking up, Conn followed the white line of the wall around the hillock until he came to a dark gap where he knew the entrance lay. It was very easy to believe that someone, or *something*, might come out from the mound.

'Legend has it that the Dagda built the Bru,' he began slowly. 'The Dagda was the first of the Great Gods and he and the Goddess Danu, his companion, made this land of Erin. He is supposed to have built the Bru as a burial place for Danu's people, the Tuatha De Danann or the People of the Goddess, Danu.

'Now you know that the De Danann were a magical race, more gods than men, who came from cities of metal and stone across the sea and ruled the land of Erin for generations. When the time of magic and the old gods finally passed, the last remaining Tuatha De Danann went into the Bru na Boinne, and there they fell into a deep sleep. And it is said that they sleep there still.'

'Have you ever seen them?' Mura breathed.

Conn shook his head. 'Never.'

'But others have,' his son protested.

'They say they have,' Conn told him gently. 'But when you've sat here through the long night, cold and hungry, you sometimes imagine things. And although this is a time of fasting, some men bring drink with them and the drink fires their imagination.' He shrugged, looking towards the mound again. 'And of course, familiar noises can change at the dead of night, and become strange and frightening.'

Mura thought about this and then nodded. 'Now tell me the truth about this place,' he said.

'I can only tell you what I learned from my own father, and he from his,' Conn began, 'but I'll leave you to make up your own mind. Our ancestors made this place, using only the crudest of tools. When they started, they could have had no idea how difficult it was going to be. Or perhaps they knew, and didn't care.'

'Did it take long to build?' Mura whispered, blinking hard, trying to ease the smarting in his eyes. He was very tired.

Conn shook his son. 'Stay awake, lad; some day you will tell this tale to your son. At least two generations worked on the Bru na Boinne. Fathers began the work and their sons finished it. I don't know how many people worked here, but there must have been many hundreds. The stone has come from the north and south of Erin, and some of the standing stones within and around the mound have been worked in the ancient symbols of the Old Faith, so stonemasons and carvers must have been here, too. Woodworkers built a frame of wood which the labourers packed with mud and gravel.

'There is a pond over there,' and Conn pointed off

to one side. 'It was once the pit from which men dug the gravel to cover this framework of stone and wood.'

'They must have taken a lot of gravel,' Mura said sleepily, squinting into the darkness towards the small pond.

His father nodded. 'They did. They dug the pit so deep that water began to seep into it, and every year the pond grows larger. In years to come, it will be a lake.'

'But how did they get the stone up here?' Mura asked.

'Carts pulled by cattle,' Conn said. 'They brought the gravel most of the way, and then the labourers carried it on their backs. The larger stones, the big slabs, were also carried on carts. When they reached the base of the hill, they were hauled up on ropes with wooden rollers beneath them.'

'But why, father, why?'

Conn was about to reply when a rough, harsh voice broke through the quiet. The accent was strange, the words unfamiliar. 'Silence,' Conn snapped. Someone passed on the elder's command, and then a second voice – softer and quieter – spoke in the Roman language, and the first speaker fell silent.

'Who are they?' Mura whispered, wide awake now.

Conn waited until he was sure the men had passed out of earshot and then said, very quietly, 'Romans, from the Land of the Britons and beyond. They have come from across the water looking for gold. They've heard of the Bru's great powers and have come to pay homage to those who dwell within it.'

Mura shifted restlessly. 'But *why* did our ancestors build the Bru?' he demanded.

'No one knows,' Conn said slowly. 'It was raised to honour the dead, and yet its building caused the downfall of the very people who had made it. For years they worked on it, living in the fields and woods around here, building their houses of straw and wood while they laboured on the huge mound. They neglected their fields and their stocks to create this place, exhausting the soil and almost wiping out the animals. And for what?' Conn asked. 'Simply to honour their dead.'

'We honour our dead, too,' Mura protested

'But we do not destroy ourselves or our land in doing so. No, I think there is a lesson in this for us: this world, this life, is just as important as the next.'

'But what makes the Bru so special?'

Conn glanced up into the sky, and then slowly rose to his feet, helping his son up. For a moment they stood, working the knots from their muscles and the stiffness from their bones, and then Conn said, 'Come, and I will show you.' He raised his tall spear high and spoke into the night. 'Come. It is time!'

More people began to move in the darkness: standing up, yawning, stretching. There was no talk now, and Mura could sense the sudden atmosphere of tension: Almost as one, small groups began moving towards the mound. The boy reached for his father's hand.

The sky was paling in the east, dawn breaking in shades of purple, blue and grey. In the light, Mura could clearly make out the tall standing stones that formed a rough half-circle around the mound. They looked like teeth sticking up from the ground, he thought. Then he saw that while the plain was dotted with people, only six, including his father and himself, had approached the Bru. And two of these were Romans, pale and nervous, despite their dark complexions.

Now they were close to the Bru, it looked enormous. This was the closest the boy had ever been to the mound and he guessed that it was easily ten times his own height. The entrance was a tall, gaping black hole in the white stones encircling the mound. The Romans stopped to look in astonishment at the huge oblong stone that lay across the threshold. It was decorated with intricate swirls, loops and spirals, which made you want to reach out and follow the patterns with your finger.

'Hurry, we haven't much time,' Conn said urgently, pausing for those few who had been chosen to go into the mound to gather around him. 'Now listen to me very carefully.' His voice was little more than a whisper, and everyone had to strain to hear what he was saying. 'I will lead the way, my son will follow me, and then each of you will follow him. Place your right hands upon each other's shoulders and use your left to feel your way. The passage before us is long. We can walk upright for most of the way, but I will tell you when to duck yours heads. And do what I say – I'll not be responsible if you crack your skulls.'

'A light,' one of the Romans said, 'can we not have a light?'

'It is forbidden,' Conn replied and turned away. 'Now, if we're all ready,' he said over his shoulder.

Mura tucked his hand into his father's belt and felt a heavy hand fall on his own shoulder. Finally, someone from behind said, 'Ready.' Then, without another word, Conn led the way into the House of the Dead.

Later, Mura would never be able to remember much of his journey into the heart of the mound. But he did remember two things – the cold, and the silence. Of the two, it was the silence which frightened him the most. All his life, Mura had been surrounded by sound, human and animal: the noise of the wind and rain, the rustle of grass and leaves, the hiss of sea on sand. Now there was nothing, only the pounding of his own heart.

It was completely black within the tunnel, and for one brief moment Mura had the idea that he was falling down a long black hole. Then he became aware of the weight of the hand on his shoulder and he squeezed his father's belt tightly, to reassure himself. He reached out with his left hand and touched cold dry stone. It was smooth in most places, but occasionally he felt lines and indentations on the standing stones. Later he would learn that some of them had been etched with spirals, triangles and lines.

Although the tunnel felt as if it might go on for ever, he knew immediately when it had ended. It was as if a great weight had been taken from his shoulders. His father stopped, Mura bumped into him, and the man behind Mura walked on his heels. The boy stretched out with his left hand, but felt nothing.

'Quickly, quickly now . . .' Moving by touch, Conn gathered the small group together with their backs to some tall smooth stones. He said simply, 'Wait.'

Mura looked around, but was unable to make out anything in the pitch black. Then he stopped, frowning and puzzled. Directly before him was a patch that seemed lighter against the darkness. Mura pressed his hands against his eyes, blinking hard, and looked again. But the greyness remained, only now it seemed even brighter.

There was something coming!

He felt his breath catch in his throat. Something was coming down the corridor, grey and formless. The ancient gods of Erin, the Dagda and Danu, the Morrigan, Angus Og, they were coming . . . Mura's heart was pounding and he found he couldn't even speak. He looked back at a greyish patch of –

There was light!

Warm light, golden light, fiery light, blazed into the chamber. Dazzling, blinding, terrifying. He might have screamed, but so did everyone else, and the chamber echoed with their cries. Then Conn's voice rang out strong and vibrant, echoing in the chamber, silencing them. 'Even here, in the heart of the House of the Dead, light still shines. This is the promise of life after death. This is the mystery of the place.'

Every year, at sunrise on Midwinter's Day, the 21st of December, the sun shines in through the entrance to Newgrange.

It is easy then to believe that the old Irish gods still live there. It is easy to believe the legend that if light ever fails to blaze in the heart of the mound, then the gods will ride out once again.

the small
dark man

*Men had worshipped pagan gods at Newgrange for gener-
ations. Yet in the year 432 AD, barely one hundred years after
Conn had showed Mura Bru na Boinne, a small, dark-skinned
man came to Ireland who was single-handedly to change its
religion.*

*He was then called simply Patrick, although later gener-
ations would call him a saint and make him the patron of
Ireland, and he brought the Christian faith to a pagan country.
So many legends have grown up around his name that it is
sometimes difficult to distinguish fact from fiction. Even now,
we know surprisingly little about the real Saint Patrick . . .*

It was a cold wet morning when Patrick returned to the
land of Erin. Dressed in a rough brown robe, he sat
in the little wood and leather boat, pulling strongly on
the oars and watching the rocky coast grow up out of
the sea. There was a smile on his long face. It had been
a cold wet morning when he had left Ireland. Then he
had been a slave escaping from a cruel master; now
he was a missionary returning to bring the word of God
to a pagan people.

He had been a boy when he was captured in a raid
on the coast of Cumberland, in the Land of the Britons,
by the fearsome pirate-king, Niall of the Nine Hostages.
At that time, many of the Irish war-lords raided the

coasts of Britain and Gaul for slaves to work in their fields, on their boats or in their armies. Along with others from his town of Clannaventa, Patrick had been taken to Erin and there sold into slavery. He had found it particularly hard. His father, Calpurnius, was a Christian and a deacon in the church, and the boy had grown up in a wealthy Roman household. His face hardened as he remembered how he had been sold into slavery to Miliuc, a chieftain of the Dalriada, and had been sent to herd sheep on Mount Slemish.

It had been a hard life. Patrick was often cold and always hungry, and in the winter he was forced to eat the scraps of vegetables left for the animals, and sleep huddled up against them for warmth. But those years had toughened him and he did not regret them now.

That time had also brought him closer to God. On that cold, stark, Irish mountain, it seemed much easier to believe in a God. He had begun talking to Him. In time he came to believe that God answered his prayers. He prayed for escape every day, every morning, noon and night. Then, six years later, the angel came . . .

Patrick smiled, remembering that wild stormy night as if it were yesterday. He had been ill for a long time with a fever, a chill, and when he had first seen the figure shining silver and white through the mist, he had imagined it to be nothing more than another delirious dream.

When he realised that the apparition was real, he became more frightened than he had ever been in his entire life. The proud face still haunted him, and he would always remember the words it spoke: 'In a cove half a night's walk to the south, there is a boat sheltering from the storm. When the storm dies, the boat sails for the Land of the Britons.'

There was never any suggestion that Patrick wouldn't be on that boat.

The captain hadn't wanted to take the half-starved, wild-eyed boy who appeared out of the night. At first the had even put out to sea without him, but something made him turn back. When the boat finally caught the wind and sailed away from the rocky coast of Antrim, Patrick remembered turning to stand in the stern to look back, never thinking that he would one day return.

Patrick took Holy Orders shortly after he returned to Britain. He knew the only life for him now was within the Church, serving God. He travelled to Gaul where he trained under St. Germanus of Auxerre and, when he was professed, he became a missionary, taking the Word of God across Gaul and back to Britain.

About two months before his return to Ireland, the dreams had started. They were always the same, and they were always vivid. Even now, with the Irish coast in sight and the wind and rain on his face, all he had to do was close his eyes to see the vision, sharp and clear . . .

There was a man in his dreams, a man whose face was vaguely familiar and whose name was Victoricus. He didn't know how he knew the name, he simply *knew* this was Victoricus. The man was dressed as a Roman but he spoke in Irish, and said he brought greetings from the people of Ireland. Then Patrick heard hundreds of people calling aloud, sounding like the surf on the beach, 'Come back to Ireland . . . Come back to Ireland . . . Come, come, come,' and the man dressed as a Roman was waving, calling him back. He had eventually realised that Victoricus was the angel who had helped him to escape from slavery on Mount Slemish.

It could only be a sign, a sign from God. Patrick had no intention of ever going back to Ireland . . . and yet surely the figure was telling him to return to teach the people about the Christ, the New God. Patrick spent a lot of time in prayer, asking God for guidance, but his only answer was the dream. Perhaps that was all the answer he needed.

So he took passage on a fishing boat and sailed with its pungent cargo back to the land of Erin.

The fishermen refused to approach too close to the shore and Patrick was forced to row the last few hundred yards to the rocky beach. As the boat crunched up on to the pebbles he wondered what sort of reception he was going to get. He pulled the boat up past the high-tide mark and looked around. The rocky beach was deserted, yet Patrick felt that someone was watching him. There was no place for anyone to hide on the beach itself, but further inland was a series of low sand dunes topped with sharp-bladed grass. Taking a deep breath, Patrick turned towards these dunes.

It was raw on the beach and his woollen robe did little to keep out the chill, but Patrick didn't feel the cold. He stopped before he reached the sand dunes, watching the grass carefully and finally spotting one tuft that wasn't moving in the wind.

'I know you're there,' he said. 'Come out and face me. I mean you no harm.'

For a few moments nothing happened. Then a small boy stood up. He was pale-haired and grey-eyed and was holding a spear almost as tall as himself. He pointed it at the stranger.

'I won't harm you,' Patrick said again.

'Who are you?' the boy asked. His expression was serious and his eyes never moved from Patrick's face.

'I am called Patrick. I am a holy man, a follower of the Christ. And who are you?'

The boy shook his head. 'If I tell you my name, you will be able to work magic against me.'

'I have no magic,' Patrick said gently.

'You said you were a holy man, and I have seen the Druids work magic,' the boy said firmly.

Patrick found he didn't have an answer to this. He too had seen the Druids perform what he could only describe as magic, and if he dismissed magic altogether, how could he explain Christian miracles? Surely they, too, were magic of a sort?

'What are you doing here?' the boy asked, taking a step closer, but still keeping the spear pointed at Patrick. He was wearing a grey-white tunic with a thick belt and there was a heavy cloak over his shoulders. The clothing was of good quality and clean, which immediately told Patrick that the boy came from a wealthy family.

'I came ashore in that boat –'

'I saw the boat. I meant, what are you doing on my father's land?'

'I did not know that it was your father's land. Perhaps if I could speak to him . . . ?' Patrick suggested.

The boy thought about this for a minute and then nodded. Without another word, he turned away and disappeared behind the dunes. Patrick strode after him, just in time to see the small figure squeeze through a hedge and into the field beyond. With a smile, he followed. There were sheep grazing in the field. They ambled over to the boy, staring at him with wide, unblinking eyes.

'You're a shepherd,' Patrick said, watching the animals.

'How did you know that?' the boy demanded, sounding almost angry.

'I used to be a shepherd myself. Not too far from here, in fact. I know how sheep act. I dare say if any other person was to walk through this field the sheep would scatter, but they're used to you. They know you mean them no harm. My own animals used to be like that.'

'Your animals?'

'Well, not my animals – although I always thought of them as mine. I was a slave, you see. I herded sheep and pigs on Slemish.'

The boy looked at him quickly, suddenly interested. 'How did you get your freedom?'

Patrick smiled. 'I escaped and sailed to Britain.'

The boy stopped. 'You escaped? And now you've come back?' he asked in astonishment. 'Why?'

'Because I was called.'

'By whom?'

'By the people of Ireland,' Patrick replied.

The boy was about to say more when they crested a slight rise. There below them was a fort. About a dozen wooden buildings surrounded a larger structure of wood and stone. A palisade, or fence, of sharpened stakes encircled the fort and a deep ditch had been dug outside that.

Now that they were away from the sea, the direction of the wind had shifted. It was blowing towards them, carrying with it all the odours from the fort. The stench of animals and humans, of grease, of burnt, rotting food and waste was disgusting after the sharp, salt tang of the sea. And yet the boy was remarkably clean. The Celts were a vain people, but Patrick knew that while they were very aware of their personal appearance and hygiene, they were not as particular about where they lived. The boy didn't even seem to notice the terrible smell.

The boy threw back his head and shouted a high-pitched 'Halloooo ...' that echoed down and around the valley. Immediately, people began appearing from the huts, long spears and short swords in their hands. A tall, grey-haired, clean-shaven man strode out to meet them. He was wearing a wool and leather shirt and bright woollen trousers, and was so like the boy that Patrick knew immediately that they were father and son. There was a tall, metal-headed spear in his hand. He stopped in the centre of the path and looked beyond Patrick at his son. Then his hard, sharp eyes moved beyond him to check the bushes and trees, in case this were some sort of trap. When he spoke, his first words were for the boy.

'I thought you were watching the sheep.' His voice was rich and strong, but there was no welcoming expression in his eyes.

'I saw this man coming ashore in a boat,' the boy said quickly. 'He says his name is Patrick and that he's an escaped slave.'

The chieftain looked at the dark-skinned man for the first time. 'Is this true?'

Patrick bowed slightly. 'My name is Patrick, and it is true I was once a slave in this land.'

'And what are you now?' the man asked curiously.

'Now I am simply a follower of the Christ.'

The man relaxed visibly and lowered his spear. 'The followers of the White Christ are not men of violence,' he said.

'You have heard of us?' Patrick asked, surprised. Although he knew that there had been previous missionaries to Erin, he had always thought that they had been unsuccessful in spreading Christ's message.

'A few seasons ago, I heard a foreign man like yourself speaking at a market. He too was a follower of the White Christ.'

'Do you remember his name?' Patrick asked.

The man frowned. 'Pall – Palladius, I think.'

'Yes, he came some years ago. He was the first of the Christian missionaries to this land.'

'There was no harm in him.' The man then looked at Patrick. 'Can the same be said about you, I wonder?'

'I am not a man of violence.'

'I did not say that you were. But I think you will bring trouble.'

Patrick smiled. 'Only to the Druids.'

'Well, I've no love for the white-robed ones.' He

smiled broadly. 'My name is Dichu. Come, eat with us, and tell us of this Christ of yours.'

Patrick's first convert to Christianity in the land of Erin was Dichu. His family followed him into the faith, then his tribesmen, and the first church Patrick founded was within Dichu's fort.

Laoghaire was king in Ireland at that time. He was the son of Niall of the Nine Hostages, the man who had taken Patrick as a slave. Laoghaire was a follower of the Old Faith, but his wife, Angras, had received Palladius the missionary when he had first arrived in Ireland. Although Laoghaire's Druids had driven Palladius from the court, Dichu thought that she might be prepared to listen to Patrick. And Patrick knew that if he could convert Angras, it would make his task much easier.

First, though, he needed to speak to the Queen and, since he would not be able to get close enough to talk to her, he had to make her come to him.

Patrick and Dichu stood on Slane Hill and looked down across the shadowed land. The stars burned sharply in a clear sky and it was bitterly cold, with frost sparkling on the stones. But even though it was a wintry night, no lights burned in the scattered forts, no fires kept out the chill.

'Everyone is waiting for the great Druid fire at Tara,' Dichu explained, pulling his woollen cloak around his shoulders, 'and it is forbidden to light a fire before the sacred flame is kindled.'

'If we were to light a fire here, it would be seen in Tara,' Patrick said quietly.

Dichu laughed. 'It would indeed. It would be seen for miles.'

'But why is the sacred flame lit in the first place?'

Dichu shrugged. 'It is the custom. It has always been

the custom. The Cold Months have passed, the Growing Season is nearly upon us. The fire symbolises light and warmth and growth.'

'And no one has ever lit a fire before the Druids?' Patrick asked.

'No one,' Dichu said, quickly adding, 'What are you planning?' And then, just as quickly, he had the answer. 'You cannot be thinking – '

'If I start a blaze,' Patrick said, 'will it bring the King and Queen here?'

'You'll bring all of Erin here,' Dichu grumbled. 'And they will all want to kill you . . . and me!'

'Let's light a fire.'

Dichu kindled the fire by cracking two stones together so that the sparks dropped down on to dry slivers of wood. The flame was tiny, little more than a glimmer – and yet in the darkness it seemed very bright indeed.

The tall man blew gently on the flames to fan them, adding tiny pieces of wood, dead grass and dried cow dung. The sharp night air was suddenly alive with the odours of scorched wood and smoke. When the fire was burning strongly, Dichu took a small leather flask from his belt. He removed the stopper and another smell joined those already on the air – that of fish. He carefully soaked a ball of wool with liquid from the flask and then dropped the wool on to the flickering flames. It caught fire instantly with a quick hiss, and Dichu added yet more fuel. Within minutes the blaze had grown stronger. Dichu stood back and emptied the rest of the liquid over the fire. With a sharp crackle the flames roared even higher. Dichu and Patrick started piling on more wood, dried grass, cow and goat dung – anything that would burn.

'What's in the flask?' Patrick shouted above the roar of the blaze.

'Fish oil,' Dichu said with a grin.

The flames were now taller than Patrick and growing all the time.

In Tara, the Archdruid and his followers, as well as Laoghaire and Angras, looked in horror at the russet-gold flames dancing on the horizon. Someone had defied the Old Religion! Laoghaire called for his horses and chariot, and then he and his Queen, along with most of the court, set out for Slane, wondering who would be so foolish, so defiant, as to light a fire that night.

On Slane Hill, Patrick put his hands on his hips and looked up at the towering beacon. 'Is that enough, do you think?' he asked.

Dichu grinned. 'Patrick, you've lit a fire that will consume all Erin.'

Patrick's fire did indeed consume all Ireland. Laoghaire never converted to Christianity, but Angras his Queen did, and most of the court at Tara followed her example. With her support, Patrick was able to go about the country, preaching. Because he had already converted the Queen, people listened to him, and he was able to convert them all the more easily.

Some of the missionaries Patrick inspired went on to bring the Word of God to the Land of the Britons, Scotland, Wales and all across Europe. When the Dark Ages swept the continent, it was those few Irish monks who kept the schools and monasteries alive, who kept the fires of knowledge burning through that grim time.

All Europe owes a debt to the small dark man.

VIKING!

Christianity brought many things to Ireland: law and order, learning and great wealth. It also brought the Vikings.

In the last years of the eighth century, the Vikings came to the coasts of Britain. They raided the island of Iona, off the coast of Scotland, and the religious community of Lindisfarne, off the Northumbrian coast, both of which had been founded by Irish monks. In the same year – 795 AD – the Viking raiders sacked Lambay Island, off the eastern coast of Ireland.

When the Vikings found out that Irish monasteries possessed gold and silver in abundance, they returned again and again, seeking treasure. They also discovered the rich Irish countryside. After the bleak mountains and harsh climate of their own country, it must have seemed like paradise.

The Vikings came to Ireland for many reasons – for plunder, adventure, and even to escape persecution themselves.

I am Gilla Padraic, a monk. Some people call me a holy man, but I am just a man, and there is little that is holy about me. I did have another name once, but that was a long time ago, before I took up holy orders and adopted the name of Gilla Padraic. It means Patrick's servant, in honour of the great man who brought Christianity to this land.

I remember the morning the Vikings came to the land

of Erin. Grey fog sat on the surface of the water like
smoke, twisting and curling in the gentle early-morning
breeze. It was not yet full light, and the sun was still
only the merest tinge of colour on the horizon, but the
day promised to be good.

I was exhausted: my eyes were sore and tired, my
muscles ached, and I felt every one of my four and fifty
years. This was the second night I had worked on into
the morning.

I was copying a gospel for presentation to a monastery
in the land of Spain, far to the south. It had to be finished
before the end of the summer season, when one of the
brothers hoped to make the journey there. Manuscripts
copied by Irish monks were very highly prized abroad,
and it was considered something of an honour to have
one of our gospels in the library. We had something
of a duty to our brothers on the continent. Many of the
European monasteries had been founded by Irish
monks, some of whom had been trained by Saint Patrick
himself, and the brothers there looked to Ireland for
guidance and support.

I disliked working at night. I sat in my small stone
cell, with the parchment spread on a board on my knees,
and the wind whistling in through cracks in the wall.
The wavering torchlight played tricks with the outlines
and patterns and it was sometimes difficult to judge
colours. The nights were often so cold that holding a
pen or brush was almost impossible, but it was quiet
at night and, since most of the brothers retired early,
there were few distractions.

So there I was, standing on the beach at that early
hour, rubbing my eyes and trying to ease my cramped
muscles as I waited for the sunrise. When the sun broke
the horizon, there was a black speck in it.

I looked away and blinked. Sometimes when I had
been working hard my eyes played tricks on me, making

dots and coloured lights appear before my eyes, and my eyesight was not generally as sharp as it had once been. I looked back across the water, but the speck was still there – and it had grown now. There was a boat on the waves, moving in fast on the tide. My heart sank when I saw its curled prow and the striped, square sail.

Vikings!

I had been in the monastery we Irish monks had founded on Iona in the year of our Lord, 795, when similar ships sailed up on to our rocky shores. That was the first time we had encountered the terrifying Viking. When the strange ships had first appeared we had gone out to greet them peaceably, but the Vikings had come ashore with fire and sword and rampaged through our monastery, stealing whatever took their fancy. They were tall, broad men, mostly blond and blue-eyed, wearing furs and leathers and carrying broad-bladed swords and iron-headed spears. We had never experienced anything like them and we were defenceless. The Vikings took what they wanted: our chalices, our relics, our shrines, the crosses. But they didn't take our books – the savage Northerners could not read and the volumes, though beautiful in themselves, were of no use to them.

Iona remained peaceful for some seven years after the Vikings' first raid, but then they returned. They stole the treasures we had managed to replace and this time they took the strongest brothers prisoner. Later, we learned that they had sold them into slavery in Britain and Gaul. I could tell you that I escaped because I was small and skinny, but in truth, I went and hid in one of the caves that lined the cliffs.

Less than four years later, the Vikings – the sea-wolves – returned again. This time we resisted as best we could, and as a result, nearly seventy of the brothers were slain. Most of the Irish monks who survived returned to the land of Erin with our abbot, the saintly Cellach, whilst others headed back to their homelands in Alba and Britain.

We thought we had left the Vikings behind. We were wrong. In the next few years they raided all along the coast of Erin, and not one monastery – not even the isolated and spartan island community of Sceilig Mhichil on the wild south-west coast of Ireland – escaped their attacks. Villages were destroyed: houses flattened, crops burned, animals either slain or stolen, and the stronger inhabitants taken prisoner to be sold into slavery.

I left Kells, where Cellach had founded his new monastery, and headed south and west into the mountainous land of Mumha. A few of the brothers came with me, hoping to find a new and secure home in one of the remote coastal villages.

We stopped for a few nights in a tiny fishing village on the south coast ... and stayed. We're still here and the small monastery we founded then has grown up around us. The village has no name; it needs none. The people tell me they know where they live. They are a wild, primitive folk who honour the Christian faith, but also pay homage to their old pagan gods. This is not unusual in the land of Erin, and often I've found that the holy places that are now claimed by the Christian faith were once similarly claimed for pagan gods.

But for all that, the brothers and myself felt secure. We worked hard in the community, we worked on the land and prepared simple herbal medicines and poultices for the sick and diseased. And because we had lived in peace for a few seasons, we forgot the Viking raiders.

The crunch of wood on sand brought me back to my senses. The Viking longship had run up on to the beach. I turned to flee – and fell on the stones slippery with seaweed. I tried to shout out a warning, but my throat was tight with fear and my mouth was dry. I couldn't even whisper. Footsteps sounded behind me and I half-turned, just as a large, rough-skinned hand hauled me to my feet by the neck of my robe. I shut my eyes and began to pray aloud.

The man then spoke to me, and his voice was soft. I opened my eyes in surprise. The warrior was tall – a head and more taller than I – with thick blond hair and a full beard. His eyes were bright blue in a face that had been deeply tanned by the sea and wind. He was wearing a woollen jerkin and trousers, and there was a broad leather belt around his waist holding a sword in a leather scabbard.

The man spoke again in the barbarous language of the Viking. I shook my head, and he responded with a few words of the Irish language. 'We bring no harm.'

I looked past the man to where others from his ship were climbing ashore. They seemed few enough, and while they were all wearing swords, the weapons were still in their scabbards. Some of the men seemed ill, wounded perhaps. Then I noticed the women and children on the boat.

The Viking saw my look of astonishment and smiled. 'Our families.'

I had never seen or heard of the Northerners travelling with their women and children; I had always thought they left them behind in their chill ice-lands, only returning to them when they had as much treasure or as many slaves as their longboats could carry.

The Viking pointed to the village beyond the beach. 'We have travelled far, we would rest.'

I nodded uncertainly, unsure how the villagers would react to this sudden appearance of the northern sea raiders. But then this was certainly not a typical group of Vikings.

'We bring no harm,' the Viking repeated.

I looked into the man's eyes ... and found myself trusting him. 'Let me go in first,' I said, tapping myself in the centre of the chest and then pointing to the village.

The Viking nodded. 'We look only for a place to rest.'

I can clearly recall turning my back on the man and walking away, and I still remember how I felt. I half-expected to get a spear in the back at any moment, or hear the sudden screaming howls of the Northerners as they bore down on the village. But nothing happened.

The whole village had by now learned of the Vikings' arrival and was waiting for me when I walked in through the palisade of sharpened stakes that surrounded the houses. They looked at me as if I was some sort of devil; I had spoken with one of the Vikings and lived.

'They are looking for a place to rest,' I said simply.

Everyone stared blankly at me, hearing my words but not understanding them. The Vikings wanted to rest?

'They have brought their womenfolk and children with them,' I added, looking around at the disbelieving faces.

Brogan, one of the oldest men in the village, stepped up and moved me away from the rest of the people. 'Have they enchanted you with their evil magic?' he asked gently.

'They used no magic on me.'

The toothless old man frowned. 'And all they want to do is rest?'

'That's what they said.'

'And you believed them?' he asked.

'Why not? If they had wanted to take this village, they could have attacked it.'

Brogan thought about this for a moment and then nodded. 'What you say is true. Bring them in – let them rest and talk.' As I turned to walk back to the beach, he added, 'And if they slay us, our blood is upon your hands.'

Later that night, when the food was finished and the men – villagers, monks and Vikings – had gathered around the fire in the long hall to talk together, we learned why this most unusual group of Northerners had sailed to Erin.

Their leader was the tall blond-haired warrior I had spoken with. His name, as far as I could make out, was Hrolf Fairhair and he was the captain of that motley group. He spoke in his own language, and one of the brothers translated for us. Yet it was only later that I learned more details and began to understand the full story.

There had been war in Europe and a new king had arisen, a fierce and powerful war-lord who swept across Gaul, driving out the native Saxons unless they adopted the ways of the New God. The Saxons were a fierce and proud people, and refused to accept the Emperor's ways. In one year alone over four thousand men, women and children had been slain in the name of this New God.

The Saxons moved northwards, heading into the cold Scandinavian countries where the old gods – Thor and Odin, Freyja and Loki – were still worshipped. But the Northlands, the home of the Viking, could not support the refugees, whose number increased as the persecutions in the south became even more harsh. And as land grew scarce, some of the Viking folk began to look with interest to the fresh green country across the seas. The first longboats set out soon afterwards . . .

What made the story all the more disturbing was that these Vikings had been persecuted by a Christian king, who condemned them because they would not follow the Christ.

I would like to say that the men, women and children from that Viking longboat settled in the village, but they did not. They sailed away on the dawn tide, heading for one of the Viking longphuirts, the fortresses that had grown up around the best harbours in the country and were controlled by the Vikings.

It is, perhaps, ironic that not too many years later, the Vikings who had settled in this land and taken Irish wives slowly but surely became Christians.

The Emperor responsible for the persecution of the pagan Saxons was Charlemagne. As they were forced northward, they drove out the native peoples of Scandinavia, forcing them to look across the water for new land. The Vikings ranged across Europe, as far south as the Mediterranean, west to Iceland and even to the east coast of America.

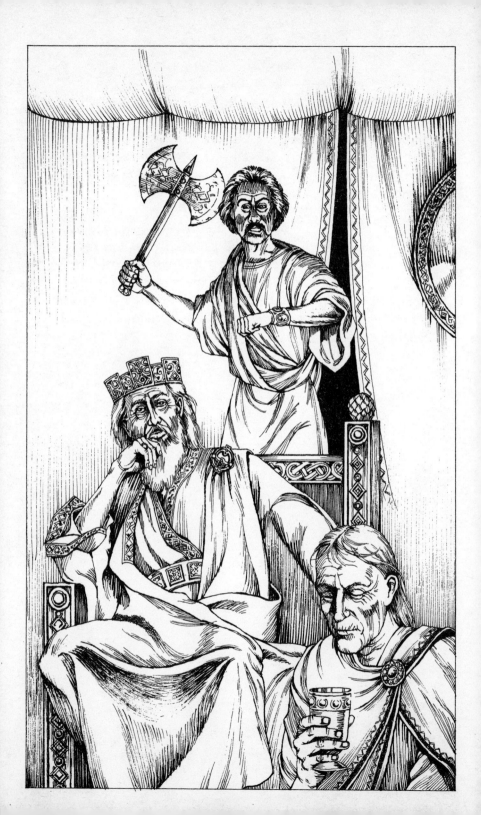

the empeROR
of the IRish

*The Viking invaders from across the sea settled in Ireland,
setting up their towns and cities along the waterways and
by the most accessible harbours. They soon became known by
their proper name: the Norse, and their influence became so
widespread that it was feared they would take over the whole
country. But in one great decisive battle, their power in Ireland
was broken forever.*

*Brian Boruma, sometimes known as Brian Boru, became
king after the death of his brother Mathgamain in the year
of our Lord, 976. From his court at Cashel, in the heart of
Ireland, he set about uniting the many warring Irish tribes.
Some were subdued by threats and violence, others by promises
of protection. His great rival was Malachi, King of Tara, but
in 1002, Malachi abdicated in favour of Brian Boru, making
him, in effect, the Emperor of the Irish.*

*The Norsemen realised that Brian Boru represented a serious
threat to their continued existence in Ireland, and so, calling
on their Irish allies, they began to band together . . .*

Sitric, the Norse king of the fortified city of Dublin, had
joined forces with Brian Boru's old enemy, Maol
Mordha, King of Leinster. He had watched the petty
chieftain Boru rise to become the High King of all Erin,
had fought him for years . . . and had always been

defeated. But not this time; this time it was going to be different.

The great Emperor of the Irish, as he was calling himself, was an old man now. He was seventy-two and even his allies were beginning to think that he could no longer keep control. His enemies were of the same opinion.

It seemed to be the perfect time to strike a blow against Brian Boru, so Sitric called for his allies. The Viking warriors returned in force to Ireland in 1014.

'Tell me about these Viking warriors,' the grey-haired old man said to Conaing, his counsellor, who was sitting by his side.

Conaing looked up at him. With the firelight dancing across his lined face, painting it red and gold, smoothing away the lines and washing the grey from his hair, it was easy to believe that the High King was a young man again. But Conaing knew better. Here they were, two old men in an age when men died young, waiting for the sunrise . . . and battle.

Smoke caught at his throat and Conaing coughed. He drank from the goblet by his side, swallowing the rough mead with an effort. Pulling the cloak tighter around his shoulders, he spoke softly, staring intently into the flames. 'Sigurd, the ruler of the Orkneys, is coming. He is a tall, broad warrior with blond hair and sharp blue eyes. He is a true Viking.'

'What brings him here?' the old man asked.

'Land, I think. I imagine Sitric has promised him the kingship of Dublin and as much of Ireland as he can capture if he defeats you.'

'He is a brave warrior?' the old man asked. 'He leads his own men?'

Conaing nodded.

'So he may die in battle,' Brian said softly.

Conaing grinned revealing a toothless jaw. 'Perhaps

that is what Sitric is hoping for. If Sigurd dies, and you are killed, then Sitric gains everything and loses nothing. I'll wager you'll not see him on the field of battle tomorrow.'

Brian shook his head. 'Aye, he'll stay behind his walled city.'

'We've taken that city once,' the counsellor said with a fierce grin, 'and when we defeat these cursed Norse, we'll take it again.'

'What about Sigurd's warriors?'

'His warriors are loyal to their leader and more eager for land than for spoils. They will fight fiercely.'

'Who else comes across the sea?' Brian asked.

Conaing pulled a disgusted face. 'Brodar.' He looked up at the High King. 'You remember him. He's a mercenary, a pirate who calls himself the King of the Danes – but not when he's at home in Denmark. He's short and slight, with a reputation for both cruelty and cowardice.'

'And his army?'

'I should think his army will be composed of men like himself – mercenaries and murderers.'

Brian smiled. 'Such men usually run when the fighting gets rough.'

Conaing nodded.

Brian stood up, his joints cracking loudly. He was getting too old for this. Tomorrow night, he promised himself, when the battle was over, he would make arrangements for his son Murchadh to take over. The old man walked out of his tent and stood looking down over the campfires dotted across the plain below. In the distance he could see Dublin, fires burning on its walls, and in the bay below the city he could make out the shapes of the Viking longboats. There seemed to be far too many of them.

Conaing joined him and they walked from the Wood

41

of Tomar, where Brian had set up his tent, towards their soldiers' camp. 'Tomorrow is not a good day for battle,' Conaing said quietly.

Brian nodded. Tomorrow was Good Friday, a holy day and not a day for battle. He had little choice, however. Most of the Vikings had come ashore and were massed on the beach and the plain below. He had to stop them from breaking up into little bands and ravaging across the countryside where it would take years to rout them out. One decisive battle was all he needed. He guessed that the Vikings knew he had lost the support of Maoil-Seachlainn, one of his greatest allies, because of a silly argument, but they probably also knew that Donnchadh, his other son, was hurrying up from Wicklow to his aid with a strong force of hardened warriors. If they arrived before the battle, the Norse knew they stood no chance.

'Will we win?' Conaing asked.

Brian smiled grimly. 'We have to. If we lose, this land of ours becomes nothing more than a Viking outpost.'

The morning of Good Friday, 1014, dawned cold and chill, with a thin grey mist creeping in and covering everything in a smoky blanket. The air was still, and even the usual dawn chorus of birds was silent.

Before the sun had risen above the horizon, Brian, with Conaing by his side, rode down into the camp to inspect his troops. He knew most of them; they were either old comrades who had fought with him down through the years, while others were younger men, the sons of old friends. Most of them carried swords, broad-bladed heavy weapons with decorated pommels, but some preferred spears, either the short jabbing spear or the longer, slender, throwing dart. A few held axes, with single-edged, broad blades and short handles, similar to the Norse weapon. Unlike the Viking, however, the Irish warriors preferred not to wear the heavy helmets or leather shirts sewn with round rings and studs which were designed to turn aside a glancing blow from knife or sword. Instead, they went into battle wearing as little as possible, carrying only their weapons. What they lacked in protection, they made up for in mobility.

After the bishops had come and blessed the gathered warriors, Brian spoke to them for the last time before battle. They all knew that many would die that day. The King walked up the low hill and then turned to face his warriors. 'This is not a time for speeches. The time for words is over, and all that is left for us now is action. You know what we fight for this day. We fight for our land, for our homes, for our children, for our future.' The first rays of the morning sun came up over the Irish Sea and turned the waters of Dublin Bay a pale, cold bronze. 'Today is Good Friday. This day, less than a thousand years ago, our Lord chose to die for his people. Today, we fight for our people. It is a good day to die.'

The Battle of Clontarf lasted all day, and it was only as the sun was beginning to sink in the west that it became clear that the Irish were victorious. They lost many fine men that day, but the Vikings also suffered huge losses. Those who did not die, fled . . .

Brodar threw himself into the bushes and lay there trembling while the savage Irish warriors hurried past. The Danish pirate was weary and terrified. The battle was lost and with it went all his chances of booty and land; if he were caught, he would lose more than that. He swallowed hard, imagining the axeman's blade against his throat. Parting the bushes, he looked around: the way was clear. If he were lucky – very lucky – he might escape back to the safety of Dublin, or even down to

the bay and his longship. He pulled off his helmet and
leather shirt to disguise himself as an Irishman and,
armed only with an axe, slid from the bushes and ran
across the battleground – straight into a small group of
Norse mercenaries!

'Kill him!'

'Cut him down!'

'It's me . . . it's Brodar,' the Viking managed to squeak
as a sword sliced through the twilight. The blade stopped
inches from his head. Brodar was pulled around so that
his face was lit up by the fires burning all over the battlefield.

'It's Brodar all right,' one of the men grunted.

'Looks like an Irishman,' grumbled someone else.

'I'm in disguise,' Brodar protested.

'Running away, more like.'

Brodar roughly shook himself free. 'This battle's done.
Now, you can stay to fight – and die. Or you can come
with me. I've a longboat ready and we can be halfway
back to Vinland before the sun is up.'

The men were all mercenaries, fighting only for
money. They all knew that there was no point in backing
a lost cause. Moments later the small group, now led
by Brodar, was making its way around the battlefield,
heading for Dublin. Their route took them into the Wood
of Tomar.

Although night had not yet fallen it was dark among
the trees, and the warriors were forced to move very
slowly and cautiously. They had almost come out at the
far side of the small wood when one of the men spotted
a light. He touched Brodar on the arm, nearly making
the man scream with fright.

'There . . . to your right . . .' the man hissed.

Brodar – still shaking with fear – looked, and stopped.
There was a light close by, the warm yellow glow of
a fire, and he could clearly smell burning wood and

leaves. This was obviously a camp ... but who would pitch camp so close to the battleground, he wondered. Moving as quietly as possible, he crept towards the source of the light. When he reached it, he couldn't believe what he saw before him ...

The tent was simple – leather stretched over a wooden frame. Brodar froze as a tall, dark-haired Irishman came around from behind the tent, followed by four others. He recognised Brian Boru's bodyguard, and realised the tent could only belong to one man. Yet even as he watched, the men turned and hurried off leaving the tent alone and unguarded.

They're going off to help their countrymen, Brodar thought, creeping closer. If the tent were empty there might be something he could steal. Pulling back the leather flap, he peered inside. He couldn't believe his eyes when he saw Brian and Conaing talking quietly together.

The Viking grinned savagely and gripped his axe tighter. With a snarl he dashed into the tent, his axe raised high ...

Brian Boru died at the Battle of Clontarf, cut down by the fleeing Brodar, who was himself slain almost immediately afterwards. But the Emperor of the Irish died knowing that his army had won: Viking influence in Ireland would never be so strong again.

queen of
the west

*In the years following the Battle of Clontarf, Ireland's history
changed dramatically. In 1166, Dermot MacMurrough, King
of Leinster, went to King Henry II of England, promising
him loyalty in return for help in overcoming his old enemy,
Tiernan O'Rourke. Henry was a Frenchman, born in
Normandy, who had little interest in England or Ireland. But
he did give permission for his subjects to travel to Ireland
to assist Dermot. Many of those who came and fought were
Henry's own people, the Normans. They were of French
descent, but had settled in England, especially along the border
with Wales. In 1171, Henry II arrived in Ireland, and the
people, Irish, Norse and Norman, acknowledged him their
king.*

*Many stories could be told about the heroes and villains
of those times, but there are few accounts of the part played
by women. In an age when powerful independent women were
rare, we find two – one Irish, one English – born within three
years of one another.*

*Grace O'Malley, the so-called Pirate Queen of Ireland, was
born in 1530, and Elizabeth, daughter of Henry VIII and Anne
Boleyn, was born in 1533. These two extraordinary women
met in 1593 for the first and only time in their long lives.*

All the ladies of the court had heard about this wild
Irish she-pirate known as Grace O'Malley, or Grany

Imallye or Granuaile. We had heard rumours that she had begged an audience with Her Most Gracious Majesty. Of course, no one believed she could dare to do such a thing – but she had. When we learned the rumours were true, no one believed that Elizabeth would agree to meet with the barbarian woman – but she had.

The court was buzzing with stories about the Irishwoman's exploits and adventures. I knew that there really was an Irish pirate queen, but that was all I knew for certain. Stories were told and retold until they turned the woman into a terrifying creature, with extraordinary powers. No one knew what to think – although the other girls naturally believed the most outrageous stories – so I went and asked my uncle, Sir William Cecil, for the truth about Grace O'Malley.

Sir William, the first Baron Burghley, was the Queen's Private Secretary. It was rumoured around the court that when the Queen had received Grace's letter, she had instructed my uncle to write back to the pirate woman with eighteen specific questions which she wanted answered. I did ask my uncle what the questions were, but he wouldn't tell me, saying his letter was for the Queen's eyes alone. So one day I crept into his chambers when I knew he was busy with the Queen. I had left one of my gloves behind on a previous visit so I had a good excuse if I was caught, but what I really wanted to do was to find the letters and papers concerning Grace O'Malley.

My uncle's study was a mess of notes, books and charts. There were single sheets of paper, leaves of parchment, rolls of paper and scrolls everywhere. But I went straight to his huge, heavy desk. I guessed that with the arrival of Grace O'Malley drawing ever closer, he would have the papers somewhere around his desk. And I was correct – the letters were spread across the dark wood. I read through them quickly, trying to make sense of the crabbed and twisted Latin letters. Unlike a lot of other girls, I could read, as long I spelled out the words slowly.

I learned a lot about Grace O'Malley in those few minutes. She had been born sometime in or around the year of our Lord, 1530, the daughter of Owen Dubhdarra, a chieftain of the Umhall Uachtarach, and Conchobhar Og Mac Conchobhair mic Maoilseachloinn. I discovered to my surprise that she had been married twice, the first time to Donal O'Flatherty in 1546, by whom she had three children. When he died she married Richard-in-Iarainn, in 1566, and she bore him one son. She also divorced him. Apparently, under their strange Irish laws, known as the Brehon Laws, if a husband or wife wishes to divorce for any reason, all they have to do is say before witnesses: 'I divorce you.' And this she did. But although she divorced her husband, she kept his castle!

Grace had terrorised the western coast of Ireland in her ships, had been captured and escaped, and had been in danger of her life on many occasions. She was clearly a strong-willed independent woman, and I couldn't help wondering what had made her petition the Queen. But as I read on, I found my answer. Our queen had sent Sir Richard Bingham to Connaught, to bring law and order to that westernmost province of Ireland. The man's methods were harsh, but successful; amongst other ploys, he had captured the pirate queen's sons and was holding them prisoner to ensure her good behaviour. Anyone else would have been fearful of bringing the hostages into danger, but not Grace O'Malley. She had written a letter of protest to the Queen, condemning Bingham and his methods and asking for the release of her sons.

And Elizabeth had asked her to come to London . . .

... Now all the court held its breath, waiting for the Irish-woman to arrive.

Her Majesty was dressed in her usual ornate fashion, in a white and ivory gown embroidered with pearls and precious stones. The huge, uncomfortable ruff beneath her chin only served to emphasise the Queen's slender body, and she kept touching the ruff with the tips of her pale, bloodless fingers. Her face had been whitened with powder, making the narrow band of orange curls that peeped from beneath her crown look very bright and her eyes very dark and fierce.

I eased my way through the crowd, determined to get a good spot close to the Queen. The court at Greenwich was crowded – everyone had come to see the barbarian woman. When I reached the Queen I moved around behind her, standing in the shadows behind the throne with the whole court spread out before me. I looked beyond the blaze of colours from the costumes, the brightness and glitter of the jewels; my eyes were on the large double doors at the end of the room. People were talking everywhere about Grace O'Malley, whispering stories about her exploits: it sounded as though the long high chamber were humming. They said she had sailed from Ireland at the helm of her own ship.

There was a sudden blast from a trumpet, and silence fell over the assembled crowd. All heads turned towards the door and even the Queen strained forwards, her eyes squinting slightly, for her sight was not as sharp as it had once been.

Suddenly, the door opened and, even as the doorman called out, 'The Lady O'Malley, from the Province of Connaught in the Kingdom of Ireland,' the woman was striding boldly into the room.

It was as if the whole court took a huge breath. Whatever we had been expecting, it wasn't this. We had been waiting for a savage – we found ourselves looking at a lady. She marched straight down the length of the room towards the Queen. I saw her clearly : a tall, broad-shouldered woman, her face deeply lined and tanned from the wind and sea. Her hair was grey and crisp, piled high on to her head and held in place with a curiously designed silver pin. We had expected her to be wearing crude clothes of skin or fur, or perhaps to have come naked – like some of the savages from the Indus or the Americas that we had previously seen in court – but she was dressed in an outfit that, although simple, was very becoming. Her dress was of yellow linen, and she wore an overdress of bright red, cut low across the bodice, with the sleeves slashed to allow the saffron gown to peep through. Her long brown cloak was lined with red and edged with fur. I thought she might have gone barefoot, but she was wearing shoes of brown leather and her feet were surprisingly small.

The woman stopped before the Queen and extended her right hand. 'I am Granuaile,' she said slowly in Spanish, a smile on her thin lips.

The Queen looked at her, fully expecting this pirate woman to bow. Instead, she repeated her name, this time using the Latin tongue, the smile never leaving her lips and her outstretched hand never wavering. Finally, after what seemed like an age, Elizabeth half rose from her chair and extended her hand, her pale fingertips barely touching Granuaile's darker fingers.

'We bid you welcome,' Elizabeth said loudly.

Granuaile nodded as if she had imagined nothing else. 'You know why I am here,' she said, still speaking Latin. 'I have come to you as one queen to another, as one woman to another, to enlist your aid.'

Everyone stopped as Granuaile addressed Her Majesty so boldly, but the Queen simply smiled and inclined her head slightly. 'We have read your letters.'

'Then you know why I am here.'

Elizabeth nodded slowly, but said, 'Tell me again.'

Granuaile continued to stare hard at the Queen's pale face. 'Two of my sons and my half-brother are being held captive by Sir Richard Bingham.'

The Queen nodded quickly. 'I am aware of that.'

'Then are you also aware of the reasons for their capture?' Granuaile demanded angrily.

No one spoke to the Queen like that! At least, no one spoke like that and lived! Everyone in the court held their breath, waiting for the Queen to order the woman's head removed for such impudence.

But when Elizabeth spoke, her voice was soft, almost gentle. 'You are not afraid to speak your mind,' she said.

'We are both women.'

The reply seemed to surprise the Queen and she took a moment to consider, before finally replying, 'Yes . . . yes . . .' She suddenly looked up, her eyes seeking and finding those of my uncle, Sir William Cecil. 'Clear the court, we would speak privately with the Lady O'Malley.'

My uncle looked questioningly at the Queen. He opened his mouth to speak when she snapped, 'Do it now!' He jumped to obey and within moments, the court was cleared of all the casual observers, leaving Queen Elizabeth and Grace O'Malley facing one another. Sir William Cecil and a few of the more senior ladies-in-waiting also remained. I should have gone, but I remained in the shadows until the room had emptied and then joined the other ladies-in-waiting as if I had every right to be there. The Queen ordered that a chair be brought for Grace and requested refreshments also: plain red wine, water and small dainty sweetmeats. Both women drank only a little wine, well watered; neither ate the food.

They began to speak. I wasn't interested in much of

what they said; content to sit behind the Queen, I watched the proud Irishwoman. In a strange way I envied her; for her freedom, her obvious confidence, her strength and her courage. I didn't doubt that it had taken great courage to march defenceless into the very heart of Elizabeth's court.

I gathered from their conversation that two of Grace's sons, Tibbot-ne-long and Murrough O'Flaherty, had been captured by Bingham, and that he was also holding her step-brother, Donal-na-Piopa. She claimed that the charges against them had been invented by Bingham. She also claimed that, since her castles had been captured by the English, and since she lived on the income from these castles and the lands surrounding them, she was entitled to some sort of maintenance from the English Government.

I watched Sir William Cecil's face as Grace recited this list, and at one point I thought he was going to burst. It was only with the greatest difficulty that he managed to refrain from breaking into the conversation. Finally, when Grace had finished, the Queen turned to my uncle. 'Are these charges true?'

The old man shook his head and rubbed his hands slowly together. 'Well, your Majesty, it is perhaps not quite as simple as the Lady O'Malley makes it seem ...'

'Give the Queen a straight answer,' Granuaile growled, startling everyone.

A quick smile touched Elizabeth's thin lips. 'Yes, we would like a straight answer.'

'There is much truth in what she says,' Cecil admitted finally.

Granuaile turned to look triumphantly at the Queen.

Elizabeth nodded. 'We will grant your requests. You will have our written order within the next few days.'

Granuaile smiled proudly.

'And in return, you will sign a pledge never to make war on us or our troops.'

I saw a strange look flit across the Irishwoman's face and, for an instant, the smile vanished. But then it returned, 'Your enemies will be mine,' Granuaile replied.

'Then it is settled,' Elizabeth said, reaching for her glass.

Suddenly Granuaile sneezed, the explosive sound catching us all unawares. One of the ladies-in-waiting giggled nervously, but I saw an opportunity to bring myself to the Queen's notice. While Granuaile was searching for a handkerchief, I stepped forward and offered her my own, a small square of the finest lace that had been made by weavers on the continent. The woman smiled at me and took it in her thick blunt fingers. She blew her nose loudly, the sound like that of an animal snoring. And then she threw my handkerchief – my expensive, delicate, lace handkerchief – into the fire!

Queen Elizabeth saw my startled look and she turned to Granuaile, frowning. 'You should have kept the handkerchief.'

'But it was soiled,' Granuaile said, surprised.

'You should have put it up your sleeve or tucked it into your belt.'

The woman shook her head quickly. 'It was dirty. Why should I carry a soiled piece of cloth around with me?'

I think I learned more about the gulf between the English and the Irish from that single sentence than from anything else. A small matter, perhaps, but it showed what a great difference in attitude and custom there was between the two countries.

Grace O'Malley did indeed achieve all she wanted when she went to London to petition Queen Elizabeth. But Sir Richard Bingham was not so swift to act upon the Queen's instructions. It took him the best part of a year to release Grace's sons and her brother, and he acted then only when she threatened to contact Elizabeth again.

Grace O'Malley remained more or less faithful to her promise to the English Queen until her death in 1603, which, by a coincidence, was also the year Elizabeth died.

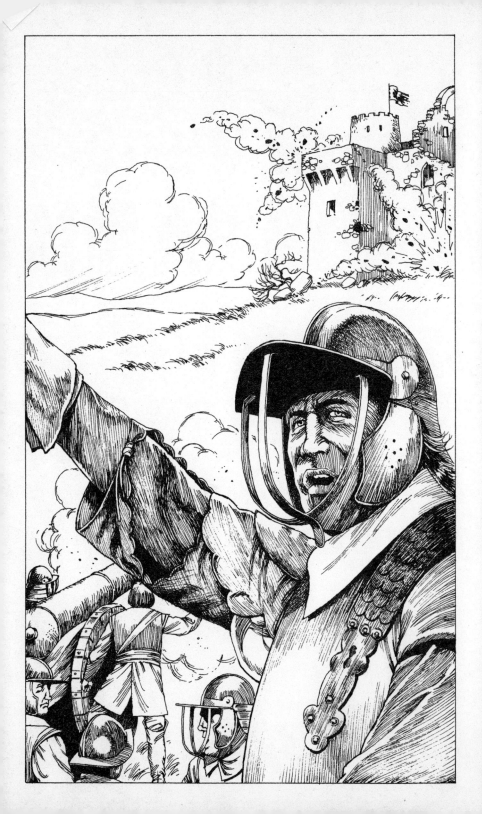

CROMWELL

Ireland's history is, and always has been, inextricably bound up with England's. Ireland was ruled by England; English was the official language and, after Queen Elizabeth's Irish Parliament in 1560, the official religion was that of the Church of England.

Elizabeth's rule contributed towards creating two classes in Ireland: the wealthy ruling class usually, though not always, Protestant English – and the vast majority of ordinary Irish people, who were Catholic, and who had little or no say in the running of the country. The Queen followed her father's example, granting land in Ireland to her followers. This process was called the 'plantations'. Groups of men loyal to the English Crown were given huge Irish estates, and in return they would protect and fortify these estates against any attack by the native Irish.

Over the years resentment of this policy grew and often exploded into violence. The English rulers and their viceroys in Ireland always crushed such outbreaks rigorously, none more so than the Lord Protector of England, Oliver Cromwell. Cromwell came to Ireland in August 1649 and left nine months later in May 1650. During those nine months he changed the course of Irish history altogether.

Cromwell said he had come to bring peace to the country, and avenge the many thousands of Protestants who had been massacred by the Catholics. Yet stories of these massacres were

*untrue. People had been killed, but rumour increased the
number of deaths out of all proportion. Cromwell did not know
that, and many people died because of his mistaken beliefs.*

The small, ugly man lay back in bed, looking uncomfortable and ill at ease because of all the people fussing
about. He threw back one of the heavy covers, kicked
it to the end of the bed . . . and sneezed!

The sudden sound brought servants rushing to the
bedside, and the patient exploded with rage. 'Leave me
be! Can you not leave me be for a few moments? Can
a man not be ill in peace?'

'Lord Protector, the physicians wish to see you again,'
one man said quietly.

Oliver Cromwell turned and glared at him. 'You keep
them away from me. Now get out. Out, all of you. Leave
me in peace.'

There was a sudden scramble for the door as the
servants left. They knew what Cromwell was like in
these moods; it was best to stay out of the way until
his bad humour passed. Only one man remained
behind. He was tall and thin, with a pale face and squinting eyes, as if he rarely went out of doors. He was simply
dressed in a plain black unornamented gown, and he
wore no jewellery, as Cromwell insisted.

The man bowed. 'If you are tired, my Lord, I can return
later, perhaps.'

'Stay where you are,' Cromwell growled. He sat himself up in bed, dragging the pillows to support his back.
Pushing strands of thin grey hair off his wrinkled forehead, he looked at the man standing before him. 'Well
sit, sit,' he snapped, 'and let us continue from where
we left off.'

The librarian and keeper of the Protector's books, for
so he was, bowed once again. He took his usual seat
beside the fire and opened the large volume he had been

carrying under his arm. Tilting it so that the light from the fire fell on the pages, he uncapped his inkhorn and slowly took out a quill pen, examining the nib. A cough from the Lord Protector made him look up, only to find Cromwell glaring at him. He remembered quickly that this was the most powerful man in England. Cromwell had come from humble beginnings to command the first English Commonwealth, after driving out the monarchy. He lived his life by the words of the Bible, and in many ways was a very simple man, direct and straightforward in his dealings. Although he had conducted his Irish campaign with utmost ruthlessness, he was not cruel.

Cromwell had never asked the librarian's name or chatted with the man. The only question he had put to him when he first arrived at the Lord Protector's chamber four days previously, had been, 'Can you write well and clearly?'

The librarian had bowed slightly and nodded. 'I can, my Lord.'

'I wish to make a record of all that I have done since God granted me the lordship of this land. This will not be some tale. I will tell you what happened and you will write it accordingly, without changing a word or adding anything.'

'Of course, my Lord.'

Cromwell had grunted as if he didn't really believe him. 'I am reminded of an artist who once painted my portrait. He did not paint me as I was, with all my spots and wrinkles, but rather as he thought I wished to see myself.'

'I have heard the tale, my Lord.'

'Well then, bear it in mind. I will tell you what happened, whether it reflects well on me or not. If there is any point which you think requires more information, do not be afraid to ask. We learn by questioning.'

'Yes, my Lord.'

Since that first meeting, the librarian had only asked the Lord Protector two questions, and they were minor points, nothing more. But he hadn't been looking forward to today. Today, the Lord Protector would be discussing his campaign in Ireland – and the librarian was Irish.

Cromwell didn't known this – in fact, no one in the country did. The man had changed his name when he came to England nearly ten years ago, having trained in the great libraries at Paris and Rome. But although he appeared to be an Englishman, his family still lived in Ireland and he thought of himself as Irish. He concealed a smile, wondering what Cromwell would think if he knew he was speaking to an Irishman. The Lord Protector had no love for the Irish, or for the Old English – Catholics living in Ireland, but of English descent. Together they had supported Charles I. Charles had made them many promises and they had supported him with arms and money in his attempt to regain the English crown. The Civil War was due in part to this, and Cromwell held Charles – and his supporters – to blame. When Cromwell drove the Irish Catholics off their land, he gave them a simple choice : 'To Hell or to Connaught'. Since Connaught was one of the poorest regions of Ireland, he had been condemning them to death.

Cromwell took a sip of water from the glass by his bed, and began. 'I came to Ireland to bring peace to that warring country. I came to Ireland to bring God to a godless people, and to protect the rights of our Protestant brothers . . .'

He paused and considered. 'I came to Ireland in the summer of the year of our Lord, 1649. August the 15th, I think the exact date was. Although this was some seven months after we had executed Charles, the royalist cause was still alive in Ireland. I brought with me some twelve thousand trained and experienced soldiers, who had fought in the Civil War here, and knew not the meaning of fear and were strong in the faith. They were loyal to me and to their God, and they had little love for the Papists.

'I was well received in Dublin by our Protestant brothers, although the Catholic townspeople did not seem overly pleased to see me.' A smile touched his lips and he added, 'But then, I don't think any Catholic Irishman was ever pleased to see me.'

The librarian bowed his head. He wasn't going to tell Cromwell that he was a Catholic. 'So I headed northwards, making towards the Ulster lands. The rebellion had started in Ulster in 1641, and thousands of our Protestant brothers were massacred by the barbarous Irish.'

The librarian coughed politely. 'I thought the reports of Protestant deaths turned out later to be untrue.'

Cromwell glowered. 'Some were – some were not.'

The librarian carried on bravely, 'I thought that many of the Protestants in Ulster had taken land from the Catholics during the reign of James I when the province was 'planted'. When the Irish rebelled in 1641 – only to be eventually defeated – some Protestants fled to Scotland and England, while many others escaped to safety in the walled towns and castles. Is that not so?'

The Lord Protector glared at him. 'Aye, and there they were starved of food and water by their besiegers, and if they ventured out they were set upon and killed.' He carried on quickly. 'When I went to Ireland, I decided I would avenge the wrongs done to our Protestant brothers. I was told that more than 300,000 Protestant men, women and children had been massacred.'

The librarian didn't comment, he merely wrote down what the Lord Protector had said. But he knew that there weren't 300,000 Protestant people in the whole of Ireland in the year 1641.

'If I could bring peace to Ulster,' Cromwell continued, 'by fire and sword if necessary, then I knew I could bring peace to the whole of Ireland. All that stood in my way was the town of Drogheda.'

The librarian gripped his quill tighter. His own brother had been killed in the fighting at Drogheda, when Cromwell had thrown nearly three-quarters of his entire force against no more than two thousand men.

'The garrison and townspeople of Drogheda refused me entry. But I was generous, perhaps more generous than I should have been. I gave them the opportunity to surrender. They refused. I asked them again and warned them that they could not hold me responsible for what might happen. But they still refused. And so we shelled the walls.' A smile drifted across his lined face. 'Ah yes, I remember that engagement well. We made a hole in the walls early in September, and I led my troops into the city soon afterwards.'

'Were not two previous attempts to enter the city beaten back?' the librarian asked Cromwell, although he already knew the answer. His brother had been killed in the final assault on the walls on September the 11th.

'There were two unsuccessful attempts,' Cromwell reluctantly agreed. 'But I led the third, victorious, assault myself.' He looked suspiciously at his scribe, and the man realised he was on very dangerous ground indeed.

'You will pardon these interruptions, sir,' he said, 'but I have done some research into this period of history so as to render your account all the more complete.'

'Oh, of course ... yes ... my memory sometimes grows dim,' Cromwell said, watching the man closely as he continued. 'The leader of the garrison, Sir Arthur Aston, surrendered to me, but I ordered the whole of the garrison to be put to the sword, including Aston. It was a good and proper judgement on them; they had killed many innocent Protestant people. And do you know,' he continued thoughtfully, 'it is sometimes necessary to kill a few to save many? I killed men in Drogheda but the other Irish garrisons, hearing how they would be treated if they went against me, surrendered. There was thus no loss of life, either English or Irish.'

The librarian turned a page, the heavy paper crackling in the silence of the room. He was sweating with the heat from the fire, but also because the Lord Protector's stories of his campaign in Ireland brought back such painful memories. It was difficult to sit calmly before this man who had killed so many, and condemned so many others to death by starvation.

'So with Ulster taken and secure, I turned south and made my way through Dublin, heading for the town of Wexford.' Cromwell stopped and looked at the librarian. 'I don't know if you are familiar with Wexford, but it lies in the south-east corner of Ireland, its weather is mild and the land around it is generally fertile; it also possesses an excellent harbour. And yet, with all these God-given gifts, it was still used by Irish pirates as a base from which to sail out and plunder English ships and settlements. I was expecting trouble there – the town had a strong garrison – yet it fell to me without a fight.'

'It was betrayed, was it not?' the librarian asked softly.

There was a long silence, until finally, very softly, Cromwell said, 'Yes. There was a man, named Sinnott or Sinnett, I believe, who was more cautious than the rest. Fearing that I would order the garrison slain, as I had done at Drogheda, he opened the gates and admitted us.' The Lord Protector smiled tightly. 'But I made an example of them. I made an example of them all.'

The librarian said nothing; he could not speak without his voice trembling and then Cromwell would be sure to suspect something. He knew that Cromwell had given orders for the garrison in Wexford to be put to the sword, as well as the townsfolk. Even the Catholic priests were slain.

'So ... there is little left to tell of my Irish campaign. My example in Wexford paid off. Through the long and bitter winter of the year of our Lord, 1649, several towns surrendered without a struggle.' Cromwell's hands moved on the bedcover, tracing out the towns on an imaginary map. 'First there was New Ross, then Youghal and Cork, and moving west, Kinsale, and finally, Bandon.'

'There was famine that year?'

'There was hunger in the land, certainly,' Cromwell said 'but my soldiers had to eat. They were fighting the good fight, they were fighting for their God.'

The librarian believed the soldiers had just been obeying orders, and he knew that some of them had been promised land in Ireland. Indeed, one of the reasons for Cromwell's campaign in Ireland was the English government's wish to take land from the Catholic landlords.

'I spent the winter in Youghal and, when the year turned, we headed northwards into the heart of the country, to Kilkenny, which had long been a centre of Catholic power in Ireland. Once again, someone with common sense allowed us to enter the town without undue bloodshed.'

Another traitor, the librarian thought, but said nothing.

'So now, with most of the country mine, I retraced my steps south, making for the town of Clonmel ...' His voice fell and he frowned. 'They did not surrender, but fought most viciously, and slew many brave Englishmen. I don't remember the name of the commander there, but I dare say he had sold his soul to the devil.'

'He was called Hugh Dubh O'Neill,' the librarian said quietly.

'What?' Cromwell demanded.

'He was called Hugh Dubh O'Neill,' the man repeated, his eyes lowered.

'And what does that foreign word "dubh" mean?'

'I think it means black, sire.'

'I'm sure it does. He was a black-hearted murderer.'

The librarian clenched his fingers round the quill pen. Hugh Dubh O'Neill had simply been defending a town surrounded by English troops; he had fought valiantly and bravely. There was no reason to call him a murderer.

'Eventually, of course, the man ran from us, skulking away in the night. When the town surrendered, I knew my task in Ireland was almost complete. And so, satisfied that I had done God's work in Ireland, I returned home to my blessed England. I left behind my son-in-law, Henry Ireton, to finish the work. Although he died in that country, he did complete his task. Ireland was ours.'

You mean its lands were yours, the librarian thought angrily, closing his book with a snap as Cromwell lay back on the bed. That's all you wanted – revenge and land. You got both.

Hugh Dubh O'Neill had actually slipped away with his men in the dead of night so as not to bring the town of Clonmel into any more danger. The townspeople managed to hold out for a few more days, to allow O'Neill and his men to make their way to Limerick, where they carried on the fight.

Cromwell's campaign in Ireland was the most destructive the country had ever seen. It changed the land in many ways shifting the population and putting the balance of power very firmly into Protestant hands.

the Battle of
the Boyne

In 1658 Cromwell the Lord Protector of England, died and two years later, the commonwealth which he had helped construct collapsed. The monarchy was re-established and Charles II was crowned in 1660. The Catholics – both Irish and Old English – had great hopes for the new king. Yet while Charles made many promises, he was reluctant to offend his English subjects and even more reluctant to order those English Protestants who had been granted land in Ireland under Cromwell, to return it to its former owners.

Charles II was a popular king. His reign was peaceful, and both England and Ireland prospered. In 1685 he died and his brother, James II, took the throne of England. This was a great cause for concern in England, and more particularly in Ireland, for James was a Catholic and most of the ruling class in Ireland were Protestant. They thought they would lose their position, land and houses to Catholics. Their fears increased when James II's son was born, another Catholic prince.

But James II also had a daughter, Mary, and she followed the Protestant faith. Mary was married to the Protestant Prince William of Orange, in the Netherlands, and in 1688 some English nobles invited William to take the throne from James. Almost 14,000 of William's men landed in England, and James II fled to the French court of the Catholic King, Louis XIV, where he plotted to regain his throne.

James II was a weak man, easily led and badly advised. He

simply wanted his throne back, and if that meant fighting in Ireland to gain control of the country and thus proceed to England, then he would do it. But what James simply couldn't understand was that, because he was a Catholic and had passed laws which gave Catholics more power, the Protestant ruling class in Ireland and England would not allow him to remain on the throne. And while they had money to hire the most experienced mercenaries and pay for the best equipment, James had to rely on charity from Louis of France and the Irish Catholics.

In the year of our Lord, 1689, in the wet and windy month of March, His Majesty James II landed in the port of Kinsale in the Kingdom of Ireland . . .

I stop, watching the ink dry on the page, as I wonder what to add. Dipping the tip of my quill into the inkhorn, I write carefully, the words scratching like mice chewing wood: '. . . With him came four hundred loyal officers of his most gracious majesty, Louis XIV of France, and our fleet with supplies and weapons for nearly 10,000 men . . .' And it still wasn't enough, I think bitterly.

A sudden sound makes me look up, my heart pounding. I reach for my sword. The noise comes again, but I recognise it this time – the distant surf pounding against the cliffs, rattling the stones together. The tide has turned and the beach below my cave is disappearing beneath the waves for another few hours. It means I am trapped here, but it also means that the chances of anyone finding me are very slim indeed.

I have been hiding in this deep cave on the west coast of Ireland for the past few weeks, since that terrible day when the Catholic and Protestant forces met on the banks of the river Boyne. When things quieten down, I intend to go up to Limerick, to join forces with Patrick Sarsfield, perhaps the greatest of the Irish commanders. But in the meantime I am occupying myself by writing down an account of all that has happened since I landed in Ireland in March of last year. All the time, I keep wondering how it can have ended like this.

The wind changes, whistling into the cave and extinguishing my candle, which leaves a smoky smell on the chill, salt air. I huddle back against the cold wall, wrapped in my tattered cloak, shivering a little now that night is falling. It is always coldest at night, with the wind whipping in from the Atlantic, finding every nook and cranny of the small cave. I daren't light a fire in case the smoke drifts outside and alerts someone, and I cannot remember the last time I ate something warm. All I've had for the past few days are the raw vegetables I've stolen from fields round about – and God knows the people are poor enough as it is without me stealing from them. Behind me I can hear the first hard, heavy drops of rain spatter against the rocks . . .

It is always raining in Ireland. It was raining when we first came ashore in Kinsale, back in the March of 1689, and even then I hated the rain. Although born in Ireland, I had spent most of my life abroad having trained briefly on the continent to be a priest. But I left the seminary and drifted into the French court, where my talent for languages – I speak eight and can write and read most of them – soon brought me to Louis xiv's attention. Because I was an outsider, with no special interests at heart, he tended to trust me, and I often acted as his messenger.

Louis xiv was one of the main reasons James ii returned to Ireland. Louis was at war with some of the European states, led by William of Orange, and he knew that if he was going to win, he would need a Catholic king on the throne of England to support him. When he decided to finance James ii's expedition to Ireland, as the first step to regaining the English throne, he chose me to accompany James. I was supposed to advise him about the Irish situation – of which I knew very little – but I would also make regular reports to Louis.

The plan was for James to take Catholic Ireland, defeat the Protestants and use Ireland as the back door into England, thus regaining his throne. That was the plan. It didn't work.

There was never a time when I really and truly believed it would work. At first everything seemed to be going well. We were received like heroes on our march from Kinsale to Dublin. My first report back to Louis was simple: 'Landed and well-received by the Irish. Proceeding to Dublin.' I think that was the only optimistic message I ever sent.

I touch the tiny roll of paper tucked into my high boot; my report of the Battle of the Boyne. I still haven't managed to send it to Louis, but I am sure he knows what happened by now.

We had no sooner landed in Ireland than there was trouble in the north and James decided to march straight to the walled city of Derry. There the inhabitants, mostly Protestant, closed the city gates against the advancing Catholic troops. James demanded that they surrender – they laughed at him.

I was standing beside James as he issued the command to surround the city. He wanted the roads blocked and the entrance to the ports of Lough Foyle closed off. He turned to me, smiled his weak, watery smile and said softly, 'We will have the city in a few days – a week at most. You can tell that to your master if you wish.'

I bowed deeply and nodded, but never sent such a report; I knew James was wrong. Derry managed to hold out for one hundred and five terrible days. There was starvation and disease in the city and many died, but we would eventually have taken Derry had not a ship carrying food and supplies broken through the barrier our troops had placed across the river Foyle. I made a note about it: 'July 28th. The English ship, the Mountjoy, has broken through to the city. We have lost.' The first we knew of this was when our sentries spotted huge bonfires burning all over the city; then the church bells began to ring out.

I am convinced that the one hundred and five days we spent laying siege to Derry cost us the war in Ireland. It gave our enemies the chance to prepare themselves, and while we sat around and did nothing, we were using up valuable supplies. Our soldiers grew bored; they had come to fight, not to sit around outside some city walls, waiting for the people to starve and then surrender. Taking matters into my own hands, I wrote to Louis requesting assistance.

The light is almost gone now and I can barely make out my rough notes. Everything happened so quickly that I've become a little confused as to when events actually occurred. I do know that shortly after the siege of Derry was broken, William of Orange's ablest general, Marshal Schomberg, landed near Belfast.

Of course, James himself was not still in the north, but had returned to the comfort of Dublin to continue his campaign. He even went so far as to summon a parliament, in the May of 1689, it was. When he told me what he was going to do, I advised against it – I was too worried we would lose the war in the north. But James needed to charge a tax to raise money for his army, and he also planned to confiscate the property belonging to William's supporters – most of the Protestant land in Ireland. Both these measures needed to be approved by parliament.

The situation became desperate in that same month, when the French reinforcements I had requested were attacked by English ships outside Bantry Bay in the south of Ireland. Although nearly two thousand troops managed to make it ashore, many didn't.

The war dragged on. It was a dirty, miserable skirmish in a country that I had come to hate. Aye, it has its beautiful scenery and historic past, but I'm afraid all I saw was the mud and blood. And the rain, always the rain. Hundreds died in that war, not all of them from wounds received in battle; hunger and disease claimed many more.

I wanted to go back to France, but Louis wouldn't allow me. I begged him for more troops. Eventually he replied, saying that he would 'exchange' trained French soldiers for Irishmen, to train in his army in France. There was no shortage of volunteers. The people knew the way the war was going – and they also knew that Irish mercenaries were always well received in the various armies on the continent.

The new men arrived in March of 1690, nearly seven thousand of them. Many were professional soldiers who had fought in Europe, and I confess I felt something like new hope when I saw their flags and standards appear. New plans were made, new tactics agreed. We began to talk again of winning.

And then on the 14th of June of this year, 1690, William of Orange himself landed in Ireland. He came ashore at Carrickfergus, and my spies reported that he had with him over 400 ships. I didn't believe it; I had to go and see for myself. But it was true: William had brought over 14,000 reinforcements for his army. I estimated that he must have had about 35,000 men under his command, while our own forces came to around 25,000.

There would be a battle, I realised, one decisive battle – all that needed to be sorted out was when and where. Less than a month later, those two questions were answered: the Protestant and Catholic armies met on the first day of July, close to a place called Oldbridge, near the town of Drogheda, in and around the river Boyne.

And what of the battle itself? An uneven struggle it was: the pick of William's men, including continental mercenaries, faced James's low-spirited army of French troops and untrained Irish. We had courage, too, but courage wasn't enough that day.

I am no soldier, so I took no part in the fighting. I stood back and watched the Jacobites being tricked into sending more than half their men upstream, thinking William was going to cross there, whereas in reality, the Williamites made their main assault below the Irish camp. Only the courage of the remaining Irish held them at bay. When William's men eventually managed to force their way across the river Boyne, I saw the waters turn red with blood.

There were heroes that day, heroes on both sides, but if any one group nearly saved the Jacobite cause, it was our cavalry. Again and again, they charged to the rescue of fellow soldiers hard-pressed by the Williamites. The battle was lost, however. I knew it almost from the start, and the men themselves realised by the early afternoon. James knew then, too – and he left the battlefield almost immediately. I later learned that he took a ship for France at Duncannon; I don't know what sort of reception he got from Louis, but I would guess that it was not a warm one.

But although the Battle of the Boyne is over, the war goes on. I'm tired now: tired of the fighting, the constant travel, the planning, the plotting. I didn't want this war, but it looks like I'm stuck here. I'll sleep now, and tomorrow I shall make my way to Limerick, where Patrick Sarsfield commands the garrison. Perhaps we can regroup and try again . . .

William of Orange and his forces besieged Limerick city. It was a long and bloody siege, and it did as much damage to William's army as James's siege of Derry had inflicted on his troops.

Limerick eventually fell, but the cost to the Williamites was severe. Under the terms of the Treaty of Limerick, many Irish soldiers went abroad to fight in the European armies. They were the first of the Wild Geese, the Irish soldiers of fortune, who fought in battles and campaigns all across Europe, in Africa and South America.

And the 1st of July – the anniversary of the Battle of the Boyne – is still commemorated. When the calendar changed to what is called the New Style, the date became the 12th – the 'Glorious Twelfth'.

famine

Many factors combined to create the terrible disaster which swept through Ireland in the middle of the nineteenth century. At least one million people died and another million emigrated to America, Canada and Australia because of the potato famine.

The potato was introduced to Ireland by Sir Walter Raleigh, who had estates in County Youghal. In less than two hundred years it had become the staple diet of the Irish peasant; it usually produced at least two crops every year, and it flourished in the thinnest and dampest of soil with little looking after. Many of the peasantry grew nothing else and the potato, along with milk or buttermilk, was their staple diet. Grain was also widely grown, but as a result of war in Europe, the price of grain had risen sharply, and so it was usually exported.

In 1842 potato blight wiped out the crop along the east coast of America and up into Canada, and in August 1845 it devastated the potato crop in the south of England. One month later it arrived in Ireland.

One final circumstance made the tragedy inevitable: the weather. 1845 was one of the wettest years on record, and crops not destroyed by the blight, rotted in the sodden ground.

The woman and her two girls watched anxiously as the wooden spade sank deep into the muddy soil. With a grunt, Sean Taylor lifted the heavy clod of earth, turning over the potato plants. Their leaves were all speckled with black spots and white mould. And then he slowly sank to his knees and plunged his hand into the wet soil. The tall man looked up into the pale faces of his wife and daughters as he lifted a handful of black pulpy tubers.

'Father,' asked Sinead, the youngest, 'where are the potatoes?'

Sean stood up slowly and allowed the rotted bulbs to fall to the ground. 'These *are* the potatoes, love,' he said, very softly. 'The blight has taken them.'

The blonde-haired, bright-eyed young girl looked at the diseased crop, remembering the large, firm, pale potatoes her father usually dug up at this time of year.

'Did you manage to save anything?' asked her mother, Deirdre, looking across the field with its long furrows now turned over, the potato plants lying flat alongside them. Beyond the stone wall that marked the boundary of their farm, she could see her neighbours, the O'Connors, also digging in their small field. Their harvest was just as pitifully small.

'I've saved nearly half of this field, and the land close to the house seems unaffected, so most of those plants are fine. We're all right for this year, but what will happen next?'

'What do you mean?' asked Maureen, the elder girl.

Sean indicated the pile of rotting potatoes on the ground. 'We usually eat half our crop and keep the other half for seed so we can grow more next year. But with such a small crop, we'll have to eat less and keep fewer potatoes back. We'll just have to hope for the best next year. We'll go hungry,' he added softly, 'and God alone help us if we have a bad winter.'

The family walked across the wet fields of their small farm, Sean and Deirdre carrying most of the potatoes they had salvaged in baskets of woven straw, while the two girls ran on ahead towards their single-roomed

cottage. Shadows chased across the ground as clouds scudded across the late-summer sky, and there was a threat of more rain on the horizon.

'What's wrong?' Deirdre asked. Sean had remained silent for too long.

Her husband looked down at the basket of potatoes on his arm. 'I'm worried. I've heard that the potato crop has been affected in nearly every part of Ireland.'

'The blight will pass,' Deirdre said reassuringly. 'It's happened before.'

'Aye, I know. And I know it can pass without too much damage. Let's hope it will this time.' He watched as a cloud washed his daughters in shadow, and shivered.

But the following year was not kind to the Taylors. The potato blight struck again, completely wiping out their meagre potato crop. Because of the shortage the year before, they had been forced to keep most of their potatoes to use as seed for the following season, and so they had not eaten well. The winter was long and harsh, and their cottage of stone and thatch, so cool and airy in summer, was bitterly cold and damp. Soon the two girls and Deirdre had developed bad coughs, while Sean grew thin and pale with the effort of working on little food. Often all he would eat for the day was a single potato, raw, with a cup of water.

Every morning he went out to stand in the middle of his small field to look at the small, twisting green plants, *willing* them to grow straight and clear. When he found the first signs of disease, he pulled up the plant and burnt it, without telling his wife. Yet he knew she and the girls often walked through the fields, anxiously looking at the emerging potato plants.

He prayed – every evening he prayed for a successful crop. Not for his sake, but for his children's. Yet he prayed without any real belief that his plea would be answered. When the time came to begin digging up the crop, he knew the yield would be a poor one. The leaves of the plants were blotched with a white fungus and speckled with ugly black spots. But he thought there might be some good tubers amongst those that had rotted in the ground, and so, shouldering his spade, he slowly walked across his two fields, looking for an unmarked plant. He found none. At the end of his fields, he stopped and leaned over the rough stone wall that separated his land from the O'Connors'. A close look revealed that their plants, too, were diseased. With a deep sigh, Sean Taylor turned back to his own land and plunged his spade into the piled earth . . .

Around noon his younger daughter, Sinead, came out to her father, carefully carrying a jug of buttermilk. She found him standing in the middle of the fields, his eyes bright with tears.

'Father . . . ?' She carefully placed the jug of milk on the ground and ran up to him, throwing her arms around his waist. 'What's wrong? What's the matter?'

He bent down, holding her in his arms and shaking his head, unable to say anything.

'It's the potatoes, isn't it?' she said.

'Yes,' he breathed finally.

'What are we going to do, Father?'

'Oh, we'll manage,' Sean said trying to make himself believe the lie.

'But what will we eat?'

Sean ruffled his daughter's fair hair. 'We'll manage,' he said, blinking his eyes quickly and brushing away the tears. He forced a smile to his lips. 'Now, are you going to help me drink this milk, eh?'

The young girl shook her head slightly. 'No, I'm not thirsty; you drink it. You've done a lot of work this morning.'

'Aye.' Sean looked around his fields. A lot of work, and nothing to show for it. He reached out and took his daughter's small hand. 'Come on, let's go home.'

Deirdre Taylor was waiting for her husband as he walked towards the muddy path that led to the door of their cottage. She knew immediately, from his expression and the fact that he was back so early, that the crop had failed completely. It was not unexpected, but it was still a shock. She had watched the blight appearing on the leaves of the potato plants, but had tried not to think about what they would do if the crop failed. What were they going to eat in the coming winter – and what would they plant next year to see them through the following winter?

She turned back into the smoky interior of the cottage and crouched down by the fire, carefully adding another few pieces of turf to the glowing flames. Behind her on a thin mattress of straw and horsehair, Maureen began coughing, deep harsh coughs that racked the young girl's thin body. Deirdre hurried over to the bed and pressed her daughter's forehead. It felt hot and moist. Maureen had been in bed for nearly two months now, weakened by the damp and the lack of food. Every day she grew weaker, and every day her cough sounded harsher. Deirdre decided she would go into the town later and buy some more medicine – although she wasn't sure if the foul-smelling liquid the local doctor gave her actually worked. She would go and see the local wise-woman instead; perhaps she might be able to recommend a cure. Maureen stopped coughing and seemed to drift off into a listless doze. Deirdre covered her with all the blankets and clothing they had and stood up as her husband and daughter appeared in the doorway.

'Mother, there's nothing,' Sinead said breathlessly.

Deirdre looked past her daughter to Sean. He shook his head briefly. 'How's Maureen?' he asked.

'Still the same,' she said sadly. 'I'm thinking I'll go to see Granny McMahon to see if she can recommend anything.'

Sean nodded. Granny McMahon knew all the country cures, which herbs cured which disease and what to rub on stings or bites, and she also arranged marriages and acted as a midwife. 'She'll be able to help,' he said, more for his wife's sake than his own.

Deirdre returned late in the afternoon, as the shadows were beginning to lengthen across the hills. She had a few mustard seeds tied up in a handkerchief, which the old woman had told her to boil in water with some other herbs until they turned into a paste. It was an old country cure for a bad cough; the strong-smelling paste would be spread on to a square of cloth and then placed on the chest. 'Granny McMahon said it never fails,' Deirdre told her husband.

'What else did the old lady say?' Sean asked, watching his wife stir all the ingredients together in the only pot they possessed.

'She said it would be a long hard winter,' Deirdre said quietly, looking across at the two girls, both sleeping peacefully now. 'A winter that will be remembered for many years to come.'

Winter came early that year, and it proved to be one of the longest and coldest ever experienced in Ireland. People huddled indoors, using what little fuel they had as sparingly as possible, living on whatever scraps of food they could find. Weakened by hunger, many died.

Maureen died early in the new year. Just when she seemed to be getting better, she was struck down by the famine fever then beginning to sweep across the land. Hungry and exhausted, the surviving Taylors could find no tears for her – she was at peace now.

As they stood around the simple grave with its cross

of two sticks lashed together, Sean looked at the cottage
that was his home and had been his father's before that,
and came to a decision. He would sell everything they
owned, beg, borrow or steal, to find the money they
needed. 'We're leaving. We're going to England and
then to America.' He looked at his wife and daughter,
both of them now pitifully thin, their eyes sunken in
their gaunt faces. It was a long time since any of them
had eaten a proper meal, and if the cold and hunger
didn't kill them soon, then the disease would. He had
heard stories of hundreds of people falling sick, and the
cities where so many had fled for refuge, were rife with
fever. He had been told of riots in the towns, of mobs
scouring the countryside looking for food, even killing
for it. How could they stay? It would mean certain death.
He nodded his head. 'Yes,' he said. 'We're going to
leave.'

'When, Father?' Sinead asked, her voice barely above
a whisper.

'Soon . . . now,' her father replied. 'It's the only chance
we've got.'

*One million people left Ireland because of the famine. In the
early days they went to Liverpool and from there to America,
but as the famine worsened, there were direct sailings from
Cork harbour to the Americas and Canada. Some of these ships
were so overcrowded and in such poor condition that they
were called 'coffin ships'. One, for example – The Larch –
set out from Liverpool with four hundred passengers; just
under three hundred arrived.*

*Wherever the Irish emigrants went, they made a lasting
impact . . . and it all happened because of the potato.*

REBELLION

Towards the end of the nineteenth century there was a great revival of interest in all things Irish. Irish poetry, plays, music and dance were performed and people wanted to find out more about the folklore of the country. In 1893 the Gaelic League was founded with the intention of keeping the Irish language alive and promoting the growth of Irish culture and an awareness of an 'Irish identity'. Political groups also sprang up which believed that Ireland should be a separate nation. Some of the groups supported non-violent political means, others decided that the only way to break free from English rule was by violence.

On Easter Monday, 1916, a small group of Irishmen and women rebelled against the British government. They took over several important buildings in Dublin and held them for nearly a week before they were forced to surrender to the British forces.

The rebellion took the British government by surprise, even though their spies had warned that something like this was going to happen. There had been threats of rebellion before, but these had proved to be merely rumours, and it was assumed that the later reports were too. The authorities did not believe there would be an uprising at that time, not while the Great War was being fought; there was a huge Irish presence fighting in the British Army in Europe. In Ireland, the timing was not right for an uprising: there was just not enough popular support for it.

The ragged urchin leaned against a lamp-post outside the Imperial Hotel in Sackville Street, idly watching a wealthy young man and woman looking into Clery's huge plate-glass windows. The large department store, the biggest in Dublin, had a fine display of crystal glasses and bowls in its front windows, all decked out with Easter ribbons and bows. It was the 24th of April, Easter Monday, 1916.

Looking up from under his battered peaked cap, the young boy watched the couple, wondering whether to ask them for a few pennies. Mick MacDermot wasn't ashamed to beg. There were seven children in his family and his father hadn't worked in three years, not since he had supported the General Strike in 1913 for better pay and conditions. Many of those who had supported the strike hadn't worked since then – no one was willing to employ 'trouble-makers', even though the strikers had had very little choice in the matter. Men who broke the strike and went to work were not looked upon kindly by their friends and neighbours. Now, Mick's mother cleaned floors in the houses of the wealthy, but the money she brought in was barely enough to feed her family, and Mick hadn't one item of clothing that wasn't patched and worn.

Coming to a decision, the boy rubbed his filthy hands against his trousers and pushed away from the lamp-post, following the couple, who had moved towards the next shop. Then the man suddenly stopped and pointed with his walking stick. Something was happening further down the street.

Mick craned his neck and was in time to see a column of men appear to the left, coming out from Abbey Street. The men swung out into Sackville Street, turned to the right and marched towards where Mick and a dozen or so other people were watching them. Most of the men were dressed in the green uniform of the Volunteers

or the blue of the Citizens' Army. Over the past months, Dubliners had grown used to seeing both companies parading through the streets.

Mick looked on as they passed. These people were a bother, with their marching and their speeches. They wanted Ireland to be free, but no one else cared. The ordinary Dublin people believed that no matter what, their lot would remain the same. The boy turned back to the couple he had been watching – and was disgusted to find that they had disappeared while he was distracted. 'Well, bad luck to you,' he muttered and was turning away when he saw trucks come around the street corner after the last of the marching men. He suddenly realised there had been quite a few Volunteers ... and all of them were armed with guns. That was unusual; they normally carried sticks instead of rifles. Perhaps this wasn't just another parade.

Mick darted across the road – one of the widest main streets in the world, he had been told – to the island in the centre and stood beside the iron rail that surrounded the huge statue of Lord Nelson. The statue towered over Sackville Street and was directly opposite the General Post Office.

Most people were ignoring the march and so Mick was able to get a good look at the three men leading it. He immediately recognised two of them: he had seen them speaking at rallies and parading their men around town. There was James Connolly, a stout man with a thick moustache, and beside him the thin, sharp-faced figure of Patrick Pearse, his uniform neatly pressed, his belts and buckles gleaming. There was another man standing beside Pearse. He was pale and looked ill; Mick didn't know him.

A shouted command drew the men up outside the Post Office. The nearest marcher was close enough for the small boy to touch, and Mick looked with interest at the man's uniform and the long, ugly-looking rifle he carried. Then a church bell tolled over the city. It was twelve noon, and Mick automatically blessed himself – the Pro-Cathedral bell was ringing out the Angelus. There was a ripple through the ranks as most of the men crossed themselves also.

Mick was strolling up to the head of the column, wondering what was going to happen next, when he suddenly saw the stout man with the moustache – Connolly – raise his sword. 'Left wheel!' he shouted into the silence after the last notes of the bell had died away. After some shuffling and turning all the men faced the impressive entrance to the huge Post Office. 'The GPO,' Connolly shouted. 'Charge!'

'It's not an exercise,' Mick said to himself, his heart beginning to pound. 'It's not an exercise, they're actually going to do it!' He had often heard his father talk about how one day the Irish people would strike a blow for their freedom, but no one, not even his father, believed it would happen now. Not while the Great War was being fought in Europe.

The men flooded into the building – some of them falling over each other in the doors – and from within Mick heard sharp popping sounds. He suddenly realised they were gunshots. There were people running out of the building now, men and women, some screaming, others looking angry. Two men strolled casually past him, one muttering, 'Vandals, hooligans.'

Mick hesitated, wondering what to do. Should he hurry home to tell his father what had happened or should he wait and see what was going to happen next? Then he jumped with fright as the windows of the building began to be broken one by one and rifles appeared. Moments later two flags appeared. One showed a gold harp on a green cloth, and there were some words in the Irish language which Mick couldn't read. The second flag was divided into three solid bars of colour: green, white and orange.

By now, a small crowd had gathered outside the building. Mick even spotted a policeman, his hands shading his eyes to look up into the blue sky. The boy was surprised that there wasn't more of an audience . . . and then he remembered that this was a holiday. Most Dubliners would be at the races or the beach.

There was a sudden flurry of movement before the Post Office entrance and then two men appeared, surrounded by an armed guard; Mick recognised Connolly by his moustache and then Pearse. The smaller man unrolled a scroll of paper and began to read. 'Irishmen and Irishwomen, in the name of God . . .'

'And then Mr Pearse began to read something about dead people and striking a blow for freedom.' Mick shrugged. 'I didn't stop to listen. I came straight home.'

'Good lad, you did well.' Matt MacDermot ran a broad hand through his son's coal-black hair. 'You did well.'

'What'll happen now, Da?' Mick asked.

His father shook his head. 'I don't know, son; it depends on how many marched out today. But I'll tell you what – we'll wait until your mother comes home, and then you and me will go down the town and see what's happening. What do you say?'

Mick's eyes sparkled. He hadn't had so much excitement since . . . well, he couldn't remember when.

'Will you fight, Da? Will you take part, eh?'

Matt smiled. 'Oh, I don't know about that, son. Let's wait and see.'

The city was full of rumours. Mick spent the rest of the day bringing his father the latest stories: St Stephens Green, a huge open park with flowers, trees, and fountains, had been taken over. A biscuit factory, the flour mills and the Four Courts – the courts of law – had also been seized.

It was heading on towards evening by the time Mick's mother returned and the boy and his father were able to set off for Sackville Street. They had already heard from Fergus, one of Mick's friends who lived on the floor above the MacDermots, about an attack on the GPO by a group of mounted soldiers, the Lancers. The boy had actually been in Sackville Street when the Lancers came riding over the cobbles. He told Mick they seemed just as surprised as everyone else that the beautiful post office building was in the hands of the rebels. There had been some confusion, but then they had lined up and charged at the building. Shots had rung out. There were all sorts of stories about what had happened then, but the way Fergus told it, three of the Lancers had fallen dead and one of them had been wounded. Two of the horses had been killed, too. Fergus then went on to tell how he had run out into the street, grabbed one of the dead men's guns and run with it over to the GPO, to hand it in to the rebels. Mick didn't believe that bit, but later on he discovered that it was true.

Fergus said that he had watched the rebels attempting to blow up the statue of Lord Nelson that stood in the centre of Sackville Street. Men had come running out of the Post Office building and piled tin cans around the base of the statue. A shot had rung out from the GPO and there was a huge explosion – but it turned out to be all flash and smoke. Later, they discovered that the rebels had made their own bombs, which turned out to be so useless they decided to throw them away before they accidentally killed one of their own men.

Before Mick and his father had reached the centre of the city, they knew something was going on. The streets were alive with shouts and laughter, and songs drifted down the alleyways.

'It sounds like a party,' Mick whispered. He was usually fearless and often walked the streets at night, watching the rich people in cars and carriages roll up to the grand hotels or theatres. But now he was suddenly glad of the presence of his father by his side.

Matt MacDermot squeezed his son's shoulder. 'Well, let's see what's happening.'

But long before they walked into Sackville Street they knew exactly what was happening. Because of the Rising, there were no police on the streets, and so the poor of Dublin had poured out from their slums and were looting the shops. Glass windows had been shattered up and down the street and merchandise lay scattered across the path, with hoards of people picking through it. Boots and shoes, lengths of cloth, coats, hats, dresses, underwear, baskets, gloves . . . the street was littered with empty boxes and scraps of paper. And there were people everywhere, hundreds of them, all loaded down with stolen goods.

'What are they doing? What's happening?' Mick breathed, watching the people with wide eyes.

Matt MacDermot made a face. 'Son, they've had nothing all their lives, and they've walked past these windows every day, looking in and wishing. And now suddenly there are no police on duty; all they have to do is break the glass and everything they ever wanted is theirs for the taking. Why, this must be like Christmas for them.' He nodded towards the Post Office. 'I'm surprised they don't do something about it, though.'

'Why should they?' Mick asked.

'It'll give the Rising a bad name. People will read in their morning newspapers that shops were looted because the rebels took over the city.'

Even as he was speaking, however, they could see movement on the roof of the GPO. Moments later, buckets of water were emptied down on to the looters below.

There were screams and shouts of anger and people scattered in all directions. They started to drift back, but more more water followed, dispersing them once more. When they returned yet again, they were careful to keep well away from the GPO. Then a volley of shots rang out, making Mick jump with fright.

'The rebels are shooting them!' he gasped.

'No.' His father squeezed his shoulder. 'They're only shooting over their heads. They won't shoot their own people, and these thieves will realise that soon.'

Another volley of shots rang out, scattering the crowd, but this time they returned even more quickly.

'Come on,' Matt said. 'We've seen enough. Let's get home.'

But Mick lingered for a moment. 'Look.' He pointed down the street to where a column of uniformed rebels was hurrying out from the GPO towards Clery's department store, which was now being looted. Once they were inside, shots rang out from the building. Seconds after that, screams and shouts could be heard as people ran out of the building, some of them chased by rebels waving long batons. 'That'll shift them,' the boy said.

His father shook his head. 'Not for long. They'll be back.'

He was right; by the time Matt and Mick had slipped away through the back streets to their home in Summerhill, the looters had moved back in to Clery's.

Mick was too excited to sleep. He lay awake, listening to the sounds drifting up from the streets below. Late in the night, fireworks and sparkling explosions flickered across the sky. Shortly after that there was a dull thump and a warm orange glow could be seen through his bedroom window. The boy hopped out of bed to stare down over the roofs of the houses to the city centre. A fire was burning there, a tall column of flame and black smoke spiralling up to the sky. He wondered which building had been set on fire. Shivering suddenly in the cold night air, he slipped back into the bed he shared with two of his brothers. The next few days were going to be interesting.

He was beginning to doze off when he heard his parents' voices from the next room. They sounded angry and he came fully awake instantly.

'You cannot . . .' His mother's voice was insistent.

'I must,' his father replied.

Mick wondered what they were arguing about. The MacDermots lived in two rooms on the top floor of a tenement in Summerhill; there was no privacy in their lives, yet Mick had rarely heard his parents arguing. The last time they had fought was back in 1913 when his father had wanted to go on strike and his mother had tried to stop him. In the end Matt, and hundreds of others, had been locked out by employers who didn't want their workers joining trade unions which had promised them better pay and conditions.

'Think of the children,' his mother was saying.

'I *am* thinking of them. I'm doing this because of them; I'm doing this for them.'

'You're wasting your time.'

'Well, at least I'll be wasting it in a good cause.' His father sounded exasperated.

'Let's hope that's all you waste,' his mother snapped, but Mick knew from her tone of voice that nothing more would be said.

He lay awake long into the night, wondering what his father was set upon doing, and finally fell asleep just as day was beginning to creep in over Dublin Bay – only to be awoken moments later by a dull chugging sound. Dozing in the warmth of the blankets, he wondered what the sound was; it was like nothing he had ever heard before. Later, he learnt that it had been a machine-gun. The British Army had arrived, and the fight for Dublin was under way.

When Mick got up that morning, he found that his father had left. He had gone to join the rebels!

Mick reached the GPO just before noon. He had expected the building to be under strict guard, but a constant stream of people were coming and going, with no one paying much attention to them. He dodged around the guards on the door and hurried into the building, looking for his father.

The place was in turmoil. The GPO had once been a still, very beautiful building, in which everyone seemed to walk calmly and talk softly. In the hustle and bustle of Dublin life, it was an oasis of quiet. But now it was noisier than the streets on a parade day. It was alive with shouts and commands, laughter and sons from men and women, banging, hammering, glass breaking, the scraping of wood and the clash of plates, the rattle of swords and knives, the clink of cups, the smell of dust and sweat, of gunpowder . . . and tea. Mick stood in the centre of the floor and felt his head begin to spin.

'You, boy, what are you doing here, eh?' The speaker was a thin man, with a pale, unsmiling face and some-thing odd about one of his eyes. He had a hat pulled down over his head which threw much of his face into shadow. The boy thought he had seen him somewhere before, and then suddenly realised he was looking at Padraic Pearse.

'I'm looking for my father,' Mick said quickly, the words coming in a rush. 'He's left us. He's run away to join the rebels . . . and my mother is afraid . . . afraid that he'll be killed and I've six brothers and sisters . . . and –'

'Now, now, don't worry yourself about it. Let's see if we can find your father for you.' Pearse's voice was gentle. He stood for a moment looking around, then raised his hand and signalled to a young man who was just coming down the stairs. 'Willy, Willy . . .' 'This is my brother, Willy. He'll help you find your father.' The two men spoke quickly together in Irish, then Pearse patted Mick on the shoulder and hurried away into the chaos.

William Pearse squatted down before Mick and looked into his eyes. The man was younger than his more famous brother, his face similarly long and thin, his eyes concerned. He spoke slowly and distinctly and when he forgot himself he tended to stutter. The other thing Mick noticed about him were his hands: they were large and rough, with white grit embedded in the creases on his palms and pale dust beneath his fingers. Mick later discovered that he was a stonemason.

'Tell me what your father looks like,' William Pearse said kindly.

'Well, sir . . .' Mick began.

'Call me Willy,' Pearse said with a smile.

Mick smiled in return. It suddenly occurred to him that this young man was probably just as frightened as he was. Taking a deep breath, he tried to describe his father as closely as possible, but was shocked to discover he only had the vaguest idea of what he looked like. Why, he had lived with Matt MacDermot all his life, but he hadn't ever really looked at him. For the first time in as long as he could remember, tears sprang to his eyes.

Willy reached out and placed both his rough hands on the boy's shoulders, squeezing them. 'Don't worry about it for the moment. Let's see if we can find him some other way.'

For the next hour Willy Pearse and Mick wandered through the devastated Post Office. Mick was shocked by the destruction and damage to the building, but was surprised by the people – they seemed so cheerful.

'Why are they so happy?' he asked Pearse as they climbed the stairs.

The young man shrugged. 'They're doing something they've always wanted to do. They're striking a blow for Irish freedom.'

'They could all be killed,' Mick said slowly, not wanting to face the fact that his father might be killed also.

'Then they would be giving their lives in the struggle for freedom.'

'They would still be dead.'

'But their children would be free.'

They found Matt MacDermot in one of the rooms at the front of the building. Willy Pearse knew immediately that Mick had found his father by the expression on the boy's face. He squeezed his shoulder once and then strolled back down the corridor, leaving them alone together.

'Da?' Mick said softly, standing in the open doorway.

Matt MacDermot looked around, his expression one of absolute amazement. He remained crouched on the floor beside the window, looking up at his son, eyes and mouth wide open. Mick was the last person Matt MacDermot expected to see in the ruined building.

Mick stared hard at his father's face, memorising every detail, every wrinkle, wondering how he could have forgotten it. He would never forget again. He looks tired, he thought, tired, but . . . well, contented almost.

Matt's first question surprised the boy. 'Does your ma know you're here?'

'No, Da,' Mick said quietly.

'Well now, do you not think you should be getting home where you belong, eh?'

'Do you not belong there yourself, Da?' Mick asked, surprising himself with the boldness of the question.

Matt turned away from his son and looked out through the shattered window. 'This is where I belong, son,' he said softly.

Mick crossed the room quickly and took his father's hand. 'Da, you belong with us. We need you. Come home – please.'

Matt ran his broad hands through his son's wild, uncombed hair. 'The movement needs me, son. It needs all of us, every man.'

'But where are the others?' Mick asked. 'Where are all the hundreds of men who were supposed to be fighting with you?'

Matt shrugged. 'They haven't come.' He shook his head slowly and sank down on to the floor beside the window. 'You see, Micky, the Rising was supposed to take place on Sunday. Everything was planned; the Volunteers and the Citizens' Army were ready to go on parade. We would have had over ten thousand men at that parade,' he added quietly. 'What a difference that would have made.'

'What happened?' Mick asked. 'Why didn't they turn up?' He sat down on the floor beside his father, his back to the wall and his feet stretched straight out in front of him.

His father shook his head sadly. 'There were two groups in the Volunteers. Those of us led by Pearse wanted to fight to gain independence for Ireland. But there were others, led by Eoin MacNeill, who preferred trying to talk and bargain. MacNeill knew nothing about the planned Rising until Saturday. When he learned about it he put ads in the newspapers and sent out orders cancelling the planned marches. We didn't know what to do, and so most of us stayed away, awaiting orders.' He stopped to listen while bullets smacked against the

wall outside, then hurried on. 'It was decided to go
ahead anyway, with Pearse and the other leaders on
his side hoping the men would come out and fight. But
with all the confusion, we Volunteers didn't know what
to do: whether to go and fight with Pearse, or follow
MacNeill's orders and stay at home. A few came out
... too few ...' Matt's voice trailed off into a whisper.
He turned to look at his son, and the boy was shocked
to find there were tears in his father's eyes. 'It could
have been different, Mick. If we had all stood firm we
could have changed the course of Irish history.'

In 1966, when the government and people of Ireland
were celebrating the fiftieth anniversary of the 1916
Rising, an elderly man watched flowers being laid in
the Garden of Remembrance. He listened to the
speeches and looked at the people around him, wondering how many of them knew what had really happened
that Easter week fifty years ago.

Michael MacDermot moved away from the crowd and
stood in the shadow of a doorway, out of the glaring
April sunshine. He thought back to that other April,
and remembered his father. His last memory of him was
on that day in 1916. They had talked together long into
the afternoon and when night fell Mick slipped away
into the darkness, heading back to Summerhill to look
after his mother, sisters and brothers.

About thirteen hundred people were killed or
wounded that week, and Matt MacDermot was one of
them.

The Easter Rising, 1916, lasted only a week. Ninety people were sentenced to death and fifteen were shot, including Patrick Pearse and his brother Willy. These executions aroused a wave of protest, to which the authorities over-reacted. They introduced martial law, threatening conscription, arresting people and holding them without trial. Suddenly, men and women who hadn't been interested in the Rising or the rebels found themselves involved.

The executed leaders of the Rising became martyrs. Two years after the unsuccessful Rising, the Sinn Fein party was returned with a huge majority in the general election of 1918. It formed a government whose priority was the foundation of the Irish Republic. But a terrible civil war was to follow and it wasn't until 1922 that the Irish Free State came into being.

timeline

Newgrange The building of Newgrange	2500 BC (?)	
	1860 BC	Construction of Stonehenge begins
	1361 BC	Tutankhamun reigns
	355	Alexander the Great born
	407	Final departure of Roman troops from Britain
The Small Dark Man St Patrick in Ireland	432	
	433	Atilla becomes ruler of the Huns
Viking! The arrival of the Vikings	794	Vikings raid Iona
	891	Alfred founds Anglo-Saxon Chronicle
The Emperor of the Irish The story of Brian Boru	1014	
	1066	Battle of Hastings
	1509	Henry VIII becomes King of England
Birth of Grace O'Malley	1530	

Timeline

	1587	Execution of Mary, Queen of Scots
Spanish Armada ships wrecked off the Irish coast	1588	
Queen of the West Grace O'Malley's visit to Queen Elizabeth	1593	
Death of Grace O'Malley	1603	Death of Elizabeth I
	1642	English Civil War
Cromwell Cromwell's campaign in Ireland	1649	Charles I executed
	1658	Death of Oliver Cromwell
	1666	Great Fire of London
	1688	William of Orange lands in England
The Battle of the Boyne The story of the Battle of the Boyne	1690	
	1789	French Revolution
	1839	Victoria becomes Queen of England
Famine Ireland's Great Famine	1846	
	1914	Outbreak of First World War
Rebellion The Easter Rising	1916	

BIBLIOGRAPHY and notes

There are many books on Irish history and legend, and the titles
mentioned below merely point the way. All the books were in
print at the time of going to press. For those interested in research
into Irish history, the following information maybe useful:

The Central Library in the Ilac Centre, Henry Street, Dublin
2, is open from Monday to Thursday, 10 am to 8 pm, and from
Friday to Saturday 10 am to 5 pm.

· The National Library in Kildare Street, Dublin 2, is open from
Monday to Thursday, 10 am to 9 pm, but from mid-July to mid-
August, closes at 5 pm. It opens from 10 am to 5 pm on Fridays
and 10 am to 1 pm on Saturdays.

The National Museum in Kildare Street, Dublin 2, is open from
Tuesday to Saturday, 10 am to 5 pm, and on Sunday from 2
pm to 5 pm.

Chapter One: Newgrange

Newgrange has always attracted attention, and Roman coins
have been found there during excavation. It lies to the north
of Dublin, and is open to the public every day during the
summer.

P. Harbison, *Guide to the National Monuments of Ireland*,
 Dublin, 1979.

M. J. & C. O'Kelly, *Newgrange, Archaeology, Art and Legend*,
 London, 1984.

Chapter Two: The Small Dark Man

Ireland boasts many places associated with Saint Patrick. Downpatrick in County Down, with its cathedral, the burial place of the saint, is well worth visiting. Croagh Patrick in County Mayo and Lough Derg are also places of pilgrimage connected with the saint.

L. & M. de Paor, *Early Christian Ireland*, Constable, London, 1958.

O. St John Gogarty, *I Follow St Patrick*, Constable, London, 1938.

R. P. C. Hanson, *St Patrick, his Origins and Career*, Oxford University Press, Oxford, 1968.

Chapter Three: Viking!

The National Museum in Dublin houses a fine collection of Viking artifacts and materials. The city itself grew out of a Viking settlement.

P. H. Sawyer, *The Age of the Vikings*, London, 1971.

G. Jones, *A History of the Vikings*, Oxford, 1968.

Chapter Four: The Emperor of the Irish

Many of the places associated with Brian Boru's struggle against the Vikings can be located today. Clontarf, where the battle was fought, is now a suburb of Dublin.

R. C Newman, *Brian Boru, King of Ireland*, Anvil Press, Cork, 1983.

F. J. Byrne, *Irish Kings and High Kings*, London, 1987.

Chapter Five: Queen of the West

Grace O'Malley was imprisoned in Dublin Castle in 1578. The Castle is open to the public from Monday to Friday, 10 am to 5 pm. Grace is supposed to be buried at Clare Island Abbey, a ruined Cistercian abbey. Rockfleet Castle, her fortress, stands above Clew Bay in County Mayo.

A. Chambers, *Granuaile: The Life and Times of Grace O'Malley*, Wolfhound, Dublin, 1979.

E. P. Meyer, *Pirate Queen: The Story of Ireland's Grania O'Malley*, Little Brown, Boston, 1961.

Chapter Six: Cromwell

All the places associated with Cromwell's campaign in Ireland can still be found and are well worth visiting. Drogheda, associated with Cromwell and the Battle of the Boyne, has many interesting ruins. It is close to Newgrange.

T. C. Barnard, *Cromwellian Ireland*, Oxford University Press, Oxford, 1975.

W. Macken, *Seek the Fair Land*, Pan, London, 1985.

Chapter Seven: The Battle of the Boyne

The site of the Battle of the Boyne can still be visited; about three miles to the west od Drogheda there is a standing stone which marks the spot where William of Orange was wounded during the battle.

E. MacLysaght, *Irish Life in the Seventeenth Century*, Dublin, 1969.

Chapter Eight: Famine

Very few places in Ireland escaped the effects of the famine, and for those interested in this sad episode of Irish history, both the National Library and the National Museum will provide excellent and invaluable material.

C. Woodham-Smith, *The Great Hunger: Ireland 1845–1849*, London, 1962.

F. S. L. Lyons, *Ireland Since the Famine*, London, 1973.

L. M. Cullen, *Life in Ireland*, London, 1968.

Chapter Nine: Rebellion

All the principal buildings associated with the 1916 Rising still exist and some are open to the public.

The General Post Office, on Dublin's O'Connell Street, is open from Monday to Saturday, 8 am to 8 pm, and on Sunday, 10.30 am to 6.30 pm.

Kilmainham Jail Historical Museum in Kilmainham is open on Wednesday and Saturday between 2 pm and 6 pm in the months of July to September, and on Sunday from 2 pm to 6 pm, from October to June.

D. Ryan, *The Rising: The Complete Story of Easter Week*, Dublin, 1957.

F. X. Martin, *Leaders and Men of the 1916 Rising*, Methuen, London, 1967.

There are several excellent general histories of Ireland, including:

T. W. Moody & F. X. Martin, *The Course of Irish History*, RTE/ Mercier, Dublin & Cork, 1984.

J. F. Lydon & M. MacCurtain, *The Gill History of Ireland*, 11 vols, Gill & Macmillan, Dublin, 1972–75

J. C. Beckett, *The Making of Modern Ireland, 1603–1923*, London, 1981.

A Short History of Ireland, London, 1981.

A. Cosgrove & E. Collins, *Helicon History of Ireland*, 10 vols, Helicon, the Educational Company of Ireland, Dublin, 1981.

IRELAND

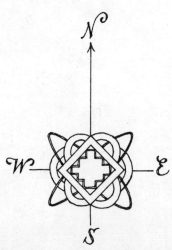